Growing Up Country

Memories of an Iowa Farm Girl

Also by Carol Bodensteiner

Fiction
Go Away Home
Simple Truth

Growing Up Country

Memories of an Iowa Farm Girl

Carol Bodensteiner

Rising Sun Press
Des Moines, Iowa

Published by Rising Sun Press
92 NE 64th St.
Des Moines, IA 50327
www.risingsunpress.com

Cover design by Sally Cooper Smith
Author Photo by James Fidler

Text set in Adobe Garamond Pro

Printed in the United States of America

Library of Congress Control Number: 2007935171

ISBN: 978-0-9797997-0-9

A version of "Making Hay" first appeared in the
July/August 2007 issue of *The Iowan* as
"The Fragrance of Iowa Summer"

*For my mom
who encouraged me
in more ways
than she ever knew*

*And for my dad
who taught me
to work hard and do it all well*

Acknowledgements

This narrative is an account of events as I remember them. The names and identifying characteristics of some people appearing in this book have been changed. I acknowledge with gratitude the support and encouragement all of the people who made this book possible. Those who read my stories, improved them and assured me that others would also want to read them: Susan Neely, Sue Caley, Sheryl DeMouth and Mark Lunde. My writing buddies— Mary Gottschalk, Diane Glass, and Mary Nilsen—who read and reread, advised and critiqued, serving as teachers, fellow students and friends on the road to completed manuscript. My friends in the dairy industry who kept dairy farmers and dairy farming top of mind and close to my heart all these years. Those 'other parents' and 'other siblings,' the members of Salem Lutheran Church. My son, Lance, who always says to me, "If you want to do it, you should just do it." My husband, David, who also grew up on a farm and was thus an invaluable technical advisor as well as a supporter through all my ups and downs. My sisters, Jane O'Leary and Sue Denter, who were my constant playmates growing up and who confirmed that, yes, we really did carry milk when we turned ten. And most of all, my thanks must end where it all began, with my father and mother, Harvey and Ruby Denter, who instilled in me the values I live by, who loved me without reservation.

Contents

Prologue

This land does not belong to our family and it has not
for three decades. After my parents sold the home place,
my contact with the land of my childhood was limited to
catching the first glimpse from the highway when we topped
a hill, pointing it out to my son or husband as we sped by
on our way to the town where my parents have lived since.
I have not set foot on the farm in ten years, but I drop in
today on a whim.

As I climb out of the car, I am greeted by the
familiar—the warm smell of manure hangs rich on the air;
the clear call of a cardinal plays across the silence; a hilltop
breeze caresses my face. Leaning back against the car, I
breathe in the place.

The man who now farms the land greets me warmly.
I know him. His parents were neighbors when I was a kid.
When I was 14, I baby sat for him and his older brother
and sister. This man lives and works on the farm, though he
works the land of other farms as well. His wife works at a
nearby hospital.

I wait while the farmer, sitting on the bench outside the back door of the house that was new when I was five, pulls on manure-caked boots and speaks with pride of the many acres he farms. He stands, settles a sweat-stained seed corn cap on his head, the bill angled to shield his face from the sun, and we head toward the barns. On the way, he acknowledges with an apologetic half-gesture that the farm isn't kept up as well as when my dad owned it.

I nod. "You have a lot on your hands."

As we walk, I look around and am saddened. The aging barns stand humbled by peeling paint and missing boards. Beef cattle look out of place to my eyes as I recall the once state-of-the-art dairy barn where we milked our cows. The farmer and I find neutral ground, talking about a barn taken in a wind storm, a now useless pit silo built by the man who had the farm before him. Inevitably, our talk turns to weather and planting crops.

"If it's okay, I'd just like to look at the fields," I say, grateful when he has to leave me to check on a cow calving in the barn.

"Sure," he says. "Look around. I'll catch up with you later."

Walking toward the west, I step across the mud puddles of a wet spring and remember squishing my bare toes in similar puddles. I don't know what I think I'll see in the field, but I am drawn there.

I put the buildings so wanting for care behind me and stand in a pasture where I used to chase butterflies. Closing my eyes, I tip my head back to catch the sun, stretching out my hands in an unconscious plea. I am open to memories rising out of the earth, pulsing through my body with a force so unexpected and strong, I struggle to stay balanced.

I see my sisters and me chasing across the field,

vying to see who will make it first to the wooden steps of the stile spanning the fence, who will be first to reach the one-room schoolhouse where I took the first eight years of my schooling. I see a tree with low limbs that I remember scrambling up just in time to escape a marauding cow. The hills where Dad took us in search of a lost cow and her new calf rise up before me. The blackberry brambles where Mom urged us to fill pails with berries she would bake into pies tug at my memory. I remember carrying milk and making hay, butchering chickens and planting the garden. All that work! Putting kids today to work like my folks did us would cause people to gasp, 'Isn't that abuse?' In truth, at the time, the work seemed more like play.

This land of my childhood releases sweet, long forgotten memories and brings me back home. Home to the farm. Home to my family. Home.

Country Hospitality

"How about a little lunch before you go?" Mom smiled at Uncle Frank and Aunt Minnie, as she stood up and headed for the kitchen. Seeing me curled up on the floor reading by the heat vent in the kitchen, Mom looped me into helping get lunch on the table. "Carol, run get a quart of peaches."

Aunt Minnie rose to follow Mom. "Let me help you get it on the table."

In the few seconds it took me to run down to the fruit cellar and back up the stairs, Mom had put a pot of coffee on to brew, laid out lunch meat and cheese with homemade bread for sandwiches, arranged a tray heaped with dill, sweet and beet pickles, and was filling a bowl of cottage cheese. At Mom's direction, Aunt Minnie lifted the good plates—the ones from the set of pastel pink dishes Mom received as a wedding present in 1942—out of the cupboard and placed them around the kitchen table. She found the silverware we used every day in the drawer by the sink.

Even though the dining room table was at the other end of the kitchen, we only used it when we had company for Sunday dinner. Lunch was at the kitchen table where we ate all of our family meals.

I handed over the quart of bright yellow peach halves Mom canned in thick syrup and brought out to serve guests. Flicking off the seal with a can opener, Mom poured the peaches into their special pink bowl, the bowl that matched the good dishes. As she motioned me to fill a plate with brownies topped with a sprinkle of sugar, Mom slid a large silver serving spoon into the peach bowl and called out, "Lunch is on the table."

Mom could put a full meal on the table faster than I could form the idea of a meal in my mind.

"Lunch"—a meal served anytime between breakfast and dinner, dinner and supper, or supper and bedtime—looked every bit like a full meal but wasn't served hot. Lunch was automatic when we had guests, whether the guests were invited or not.

Relatives like Uncle Frank and Aunt Minnie dropped in to visit on Sunday afternoon. We had lunch before they left. Friends showed up to play cards on Friday night. We had lunch before they went home to bed. Women came for a Homemaker's meeting, Mom served lunch. Even if our guests had eaten a full dinner or supper meal only hours before, we still served and guests still ate lunch. And it wasn't just us. When we went visiting, we were served lunch. Any visit by anyone to our farm, any visit by us to any other farm was occasion to set the coffee pot to perking on the stove and to bring, at the very least, a plate of cookies to the table. This was farm hospitality.

Beyond satisfying any real or imagined hunger pangs our guests might have, serving lunch provided an unspoken signal that it was time for people to go home so we could go out and do chores or go to bed. No one ever missed the hint that it was time to leave. How could you be offended when your hosts sent you on your way with a full tummy?

Nor would you refuse an offer of lunch. The general rule was that if lunch was offered, you settled in at the table, shared neighborhood news, and ate.

It's fair to say that not all lunches were created equal. Visiting some neighbors and having lunch was a treat akin to getting candy at Easter, the food was so amazing. An older neighbor who lived a couple miles east of us topped the list in this category, and what she served was even more amazing to me because of her stove.

Edna Hoffman cooked on a wood-burning cookstove so big it filled the end of her kitchen. She fed the fire in the cookstove with pieces of wood her husband George had split from logs and piled in a wood box near the stove. Though electricity was available in rural Iowa by the mid-1940s and most families had abandoned cookstoves at that time, Edna swore by hers and kept it as long as she was on the farm, well into the 1970s.

That cookstove offered a fascinating array of doors and burner lids. Flames danced behind each door, under each lid. A small cupboard above the burners was a warming oven, a cozy place to remove the chill from plates, to keep a side dish hot while other dishes cooked, or to rewarm dinner rolls. Mom gazed with envy at that warming oven each time we visited Edna's kitchen and remembered it fondly decades later.

Only a cookstove expert like Edna could manage the variable heat of open flames to turn out culinary magic. One time she presented a Baked Alaska combining white cake topped with ice cream that hadn't melted even though it came right out of the oven beneath a mountain of meringue tinged a perfect brown. Another time, light-as-air cream puffs came out of her cookstove. Filled with ice cream, topped with fresh red raspberries, and drizzled over with chocolate syrup, those cream puffs were as good as any dessert I'd eaten up until then or have since.

We visited other neighbors more often and with mixed results when it came to lunch. It was on one of these visits that I learned an important lesson in hospitality.

Bob 'n Tot Richardson were neighbors we saw frequently because Dad rented hay ground from them. I think they were also some sort of shirttail relation, but even though Mom explained repeatedly how this person or that person in the neighborhood was related to someone else, I could never keep it straight.

I never thought of Bob 'n Tot independently of each other. Dad never said, "We're going over to Tot's," or "I need to go see Bob." It was always, "We're going to see Bob 'n Tot."

Bob looked like a smaller, older version of Dad. He wore the standard farmer uniform, dark blue denim pants and a light blue chambray shirt, a blue or red farmer's kerchief folded in his back pocket. I bet when he emptied his pockets, he dumped out nails and change, pliers and a pocket knife just like Dad carried around.

Tot was a short woman with salt-and-pepper gray in her brown hair. Though she repeatedly tucked her hair into a bun at the nape of her neck, strands worked their way loose, flying along in her energetic wake.

Tot's house was a refuge for ailing baby birds and animals of all sorts. There were chickens in the yard and in the spring we'd often find baby chicks being kept warm in her oven.

At our house, our dog Butch could come into the kitchen but no further. Other than the periodic parakeet or goldfish, Mom and Dad allowed no other animals, so going to Tot's house was a journey into the unexpected.

One time Tot had a baby robin she was nursing back to health. We watched as she fed it a tiny piece of raw hamburger. Then a fresh raspberry. "Isn't that the damnedest thing?" she chortled as the robin opened up its beak wide every time she brought it a little food. The next time we came to visit, I asked about the robin. Tot's smile turned into a frown. "You won't believe it," she said. "One day that robin flew over to the toilet. I guess it wanted a drink. It fell in and drowned."

"Oohhh," I moaned. "What did you do?"

Tot shrugged practical shoulders. "Flushed it down."

It was usually more interesting to visit when the neighbors had kids our age. Then we'd be off exploring their barns and checking out their animals. But even though Bob 'n Tot never had kids, I still never much minded a visit to their place. Bob 'n Tot were the only people I knew who raised sheep. On each visit, I wandered past the sheep pasture where I worked my fingers through the curly tight, gray-white wool on the back of one of the sheep crowded by the fence. For the rest of the day, I marveled at the curious lanolin oily softness that coated my hands.

One day Dad needed to talk with Bob about the hay ground, so we all piled into the Chevrolet sedan and went along. After a stop to check out the sheep, my sister Sue and I followed Mom to the house.

Tot was at the door to greet us even before we knocked. "Come on in," she urged, opening the door wide to welcome us into her kitchen while she held Coco back with one foot.

A little brown, yappy Chihuahua, Coco raced

around the house like a crazed lunatic, his eyes bugged out, toenails clicking, skinny legs sliding on the kitchen linoleum. We edged into the kitchen, giving Coco a wide berth. An irritable bundle of nervous energy, Coco would like as not bite any hand that came close.

"Coco, be quiet!" Tot scolded as the dog careened by. "That damn dog," she added, shaking her head as though there was not a single thing she could do.

Tot talked a hundred miles an hour and she was the only woman in my acquaintance who swore. And she let it rip just like a man. Mom never, ever, let a swear word pass her lips. Whenever Tot swore, which was every time we saw her, I watched Mom out of the corner of my eye, waiting for a reaction. Mom never even twitched.

"You girls take a look at what I have on the porch," Tot pointed us toward a box bathed in the sunshine streaming through the window.

"Kittens!" I said as Sue and I crouched by the box where a mother cat lay with five baby kittens latched to her teats. "Look! They don't even have their eyes open yet." Even with their eyes closed, the kittens found their way to milk and lay flexing their paws, kneading their mama like she was bread dough.

"Can we hold them?" Sue looked up at Tot and Mom.

Tot bent over our shoulders. "Better not. They're too little yet, They were just born day before yesterday. You can touch them, but just a little."

I trailed a finger along the back of one of the mouse-sized kittens with fur that felt like silk. Sue did the same. "They're so soft," I crooned.

"Better leave them alone now," Mom said. "You'll make the mama nervous."

"The men will be awhile," Tot said. "I'm going to put the coffee on. Why don't you girls go in the living room and see if there's anything there that interests you."

"Don't touch anything," Mom warned.

Now how conflicting was that advice? Find something interesting, but don't touch it. We'd been in Tot's living room before. Mom didn't have a lot to be worried about.

"Look at the dog hair," Sue whispered when we rounded the corner from kitchen to living room. It was obvious Coco had free access to the furniture. Every inch of every chair and the couch was covered with fine, brown dog hairs.

"Shh." I touched a finger to my lips. "You don't want her to hear." We worked our way around the living room, looking at knickknacks on the TV and shelves, but touching nothing, an assignment that held our interest for about two minutes. Eyeing the dog hair, we didn't even consider asking about TV. Neither of us wanted to sit down.

It did not take long for us to find ourselves back in the kitchen where we slid onto kitchen chairs. The red plastic seats were cool against my legs.

Mom and Tot sat sipping steaming coffee from brimming cups as I watched with envy. I looked forward to being old enough to drink coffee.

"Have a cookie." Tot slid a plate stacked with date cookies across the table to Sue and me. Then she popped out of her chair. "Say, would you girls like some hot chocolate?" Tot was up rummaging in the cupboards for a pan before we could answer.

"That'd be great." I perked up. I loved hot chocolate. At our house, we only had hot chocolate in the winter. This would be a treat. Maybe Tot would have marshmallows, too. Miniature marshmallows would be fun.

Tot bustled around the kitchen making the hot chocolate. Meanwhile, I tilted from side to side on my chair, enjoying the feel of peeling the skin of one bare leg off the plastic seat and then rocking over to peel the other leg off the seat. I looked at Sue; she was doing the same thing. When we giggled, Mom put her hand on my shoulder. Behind her smile we heard meaning. We sat still.

Pretty soon, Tot set a cup of steaming cocoa in front of each of us girls. I stifled a sigh. No marshmallows. "Thank you," Sue and I said at the same time. We'd been taught well.

I lifted the cup in both hands and brought it close to my lips. It was too hot to drink so I blew little puffs across the surface, just the way I saw Mom blow across a just-poured cup of coffee. Sue did the same thing. The liquid was dark brown and smelled deliciously chocolate.

I took a little sip. And almost gagged. I glanced at Sue; she had a sick look on her face. I looked at Mom, who had seen our reaction. The look in her eyes said, "Don't say anything."

Tentatively, I lifted the cup again. Maybe it got better as it cooled. But it didn't. My throat locked closed as the bitter liquid crossed my tongue and headed toward my stomach. What was this stuff? And how was I going to drink it?

Tot sat back down at the table and picked up her coffee cup. "How is it?" she asked, looking right at me. Perhaps I was not as green as I felt.

What could I say? Panic rose in my throat along with bile from the sip of cocoa. "It's good," I squeaked, forcing a little smile. Mom nodded at me and visibly relaxed.

Tot smiled and went on talking with Mom about gardens and canning. While they talked, I tried to figure out what had gone wrong with something as simple as hot cocoa. Sue nudged my leg with her toe. I peeked at her out of the corner of my eye, saw the panic in her wide, brown eyes, shrugged my shoulder a half-inch and looked back at my cup. We were trapped. I thought again about marshmallows. They might make it better. But I was afraid to ask. And what was I going to say? *This cocoa is terrible and maybe marshmallows would save it?*

I took sip after painful sip from what had become a bottomless cup. Maybe I could say I wasn't thirsty after all. Maybe I would throw up. Maybe I would get sick and die. But I couldn't NOT drink the cocoa either. So I drank. And with each sip, my throat tightened, feeling more and more like the year I got the mumps and could barely swallow at all for two whole weeks.

When I drained the last bit of cocoa from my cup, Tot asked, "Would you like more?" She was already on her feet heading for the stove.

"NO, THANKS!" The words exploded from my mouth. Tot jumped. She whirled toward me with a puzzled look. "No." I forced another smile. "Thanks. I'm full."

"I see Harvey coming," Mom said out of the blue as she stood up and motioned us to the door. "Girls. Are you ready to go?" She didn't need to ask twice. Sue and I were off our chairs and headed for the door. "Thanks for the coffee and hot chocolate, Tot," Mom added. "You'll have to come visit us soon."

Safe in the car, I complained, "Mom, that hot chocolate was awful. I don't know what it was, but I thought I was going to get sick."

Holding her stomach, Sue rolled onto her side in the back seat, "Yeah, I thought I would throw up!"

"Now I'm sure it wasn't so bad," Mom said.

"It was, too," I insisted. "It was disgusting! Don't you think Tot would know how to make cocoa?" I ran my tongue across the top of my mouth and scraped it on my front teeth to destroy the lingering bitter taste.

"I'm sure she does," Mom said. "But I don't think she had any milk in the house. That's why she made it with hot water. And I saw her use cocoa powder. That's not sweetened."

Hot water and cocoa powder? Not milk and Nestlés Quik!

"I'm sure she didn't know how that would taste," Mom continued. "And she wanted to have something for you girls. It was nice of her to offer, and it was the right thing to drink it. I'm proud of you."

I scraped my tongue across my teeth again. In all the times I had seen Mom offer food and watched guests eat that food, in all the times neighbors had offered us food and we'd eaten that food, it had never occurred to me that the food might not be good. And that people would still eat it. And then say, "Thanks." I had just never imagined that this, too, was a part of hospitality.

Sunday Dinner

"Why do we have chicken for dinner *every* Sunday?" I asked Mom one Sunday morning.

She glanced at me with a look that suggested I might be daft and said, "Because we have them." Then she slipped another chicken leg into the hot grease. When she looked back to find me still looking up at her, she said, "Now go get ready for church. Dad will be ready to go and we don't want to keep him waiting."

I stared at her for a second more, then headed for the bedroom, pulling off my shirt on the way. Well of course we have chickens, I thought. *How* could a farm exist without chickens?

Eating fried chicken with mashed potatoes and gravy marked our Sundays as certainly as did sitting in the fourth pew on the left side of the aisle at Salem Lutheran Church in Spragueville, Iowa.

We filed into that pew because every Sunday morning after Dad put on his suit, straightened his tie and donned his gray fedora, he strode without hesitation to the car, proclaiming so we would all hear: "The bus is leaving! Get a move on. We don't want to be sitting in the preacher's lap." Dressed in our go-to-church dresses and the black patent leather shoes bought new each year for Easter Sunday, we hustled out to the car before he had a chance to lay on the horn.

We had fried chicken every single Sunday except for Thanksgiving or Christmas or Easter, when we had turkey or ham.

We ate eggs for breakfast every day, except Sunday when we had cold cereal. On every other day, eggs—fried, scrambled, poached or boiled—followed oatmeal and accompanied pancakes.

Mom used eggs to bake cakes, cookies, dumplings dropped by the spoonful into tomato soup, noodles that hung in even rows like pieces of twine on the backs of chairs—to bake, well, just everything.

We ate eggs, we ate chicken. Of course we had chickens.

It always amazed me that you could go to a feed store and buy little living balls of yellow fluff baby chicks just the same as you could buy onion sets and sweet corn seed when it was time to plant the garden. But you could, and each spring Dad brought home boxes of baby chicks from the feed store in Preston. As he unloaded the boxes from the truck seat and carried them in the house, we heard the anxious 'cheep, cheep, cheeps' and saw little beaks poking through the air holes punched all around the box.

In a small pen in a corner of the basement, Dad rigged up a heat lamp to keep their tiny bodies warm. Mom dug out the quart jar waterer and a tray of feed. Crouching shoulder to shoulder between the box and the pen, we kids gathered each bitty, cheeping fluff ball out of the box, cradling it carefully in our hands, giggling as their feet tickled our palms.

We dipped each chick's beak in the water so it would know to drink, then set it under the heat lamp. The chicks huddled together under the warm circle of light, one or two breaking off every little while to run for a drink and then returning to the warmth and safety of the wriggling, yellow mass. Each morning, we raced to the basement to refresh the water and add feed to the tray.

Chicks grow very quickly so we only had them in the basement for a week or so before white feathers replaced yellow down. Then we moved them to the chicken coop where they joined the hens from last year's box of chicks. Within a couple of weeks, we could begin to see which birds would be pullets and which roosters. Within six to eight weeks, roosters were ready to be eaten and pullets to lay eggs.

In each 'straight run' box of 100 Leghorn chicks, there were about 70 roosters and 30 hens. As they grew up, it was easier to spot which was which. The roosters developed bright red combs on their heads, strutted around like they knew something important, and crowed as they scratched the ground and ate. The pullets with their neat little combs, clucked and scratched, all business as they set about laying eggs, eggs that were at first half the size of a regular egg. These miniature-sized pullet eggs seemed like they should be used to feed our dolls.

We raised the chickens, we collected the eggs, we ate eggs and sold the surplus, and we butchered the chickens to eat.

As I mentioned, Mom fried a chicken every Sunday for dinner.

On Saturday night as soon as the supper dishes

were done, Mom took a frozen chicken from the basement deep freeze and set it to thaw in the kitchen sink. (This was before anyone counseled against thawing meat at room temperature. Since none of us ever got sick, this caution is one I would only half pay attention to myself when I was grown.)

After the breakfast dishes were done and before we took off for church, Mom put an apron over her Sunday dress, dredged each piece of chicken in flour and placed it in a half-inch of hot oil in the black cast-iron skillet. There it turned a rich, oaken color. After each piece was perfectly browned, she put all the chicken in a Dutch oven and slid it into the oven to cook on low heat. By that time the house was saturated in a smell so wonderful my stomach growled. I was hungry again, and it didn't matter that I had just finished breakfast. When we returned from church, we were all truly hungry, and that falling-off-the-bone tender chicken was ready to put on a platter, the drippings ready to make gravy. The only thing we had to wait on was potatoes to boil. To a kid that was an intolerably long wait.

A chicken every Sunday for our family of six, including Grandma, meant 50 to 52 chickens. Often we had company for dinner on Sunday—Aunt Joyce and Uncle Ed, plus our four cousins, or the Pastor and his wife, or on rarer occasions our relatives on Dad's side from Wisconsin. On days when company joined us, fried chicken dinner took more than one chicken. Just do the math. Mom could easily have to retrieve 70 or more chickens in a year out of the freezer.

If we ran out of chickens in the freezer, Mom would say to Dad, "We need a chicken for dinner." Then—before he headed down the hill to do barn chores—Dad lifted an ax off the hook by his workbench in the garage, detoured to the coop, and dispatched a rooster in about one second on a block just outside the chicken coop door. Mom took over from there, scalding the chicken in a pot of boiling water on the gas stove in the basement, plucking the feathers, gutting, cleaning and cutting up the chicken to fry. Chicken house to table took a couple of hours. We were part of the Fresh Food Movement long before it became popular.

When Dad wasn't around, Mom could kill a chicken, and from time to time she did, but she wasn't wild about it. Grandma Denter—Dad's mom—had no such qualms. When she stayed with us in the fall after school started, she never hesitated to pick up the ax, grab the long wire hook and hook the first rooster leg to pass within snagging distance. So accustomed was she to the task that she seldom got a drop of blood on the apron that covered her ample figure.

But usually, killing chickens was Dad's job.

Most chickens made it to the dinner table in that traditional way, but there was one exception.

One Easter, someone gave a chick to my cousins who lived in Sabula, a small town on an island in the Mississippi River. Pretty quick the chick grew into a rooster and Aunt Joyce decided they couldn't keep it in town any more so that rooster came to live on our farm. We could see right away why Aunt Joyce didn't want it around. That bird was feisty.

One day soon after the rooster arrived, Sue and I were out playing in the yard. My sister Sue was a tiny thing with big brown eyes and white blond hair. How that big white king-of-the-coop rooster could see Sue as a threat to his yard is beyond me, but he did. Out of nowhere he came, crowing and flapping his wings, heading straight at Sue.

Sue screamed. I screamed. The rooster flew away and then came back again. He pecked at her head, jabbed her with his claws, beat her with his wings. Sue screamed and flailed her arms, succeeding only in making the rooster more angry. She was no match. And what did I do while my sister was being bloodied by the rooster? I did the only thing I could think to do; I ran for the house.

"Dad! Mom! The rooster is killing Sue," I shrieked, my heart thudding so loud I could hear it in my ears, my face whiter than the rooster's feathers.

Dad was out of the house in less time than I could take a breath. Mom was right behind him. Dad grabbed the rooster by the head and flung it around in a big loop, snapping the bird's neck before he let it loose to tumble across the lawn. Mom scooped up Sue and whisked her into the house. We had that rooster for supper.

Getting the new crop of roosters into the freezer each fall took all of us working at it for the better part of one full day.

"We're butchering chickens today," Mom would announce one day as she pulled her largest kettles out of the cupboards, filled them with water and set them to boiling on the basement stove. "You girls go help Dad."

Scampering out of the house, we trailed Dad to the chicken house. "Tooter, you and Squirt snag them and hand them out," he said as he handed my sister Jane and me long wires with the ends bent into hooks. "Bugs, you hold 'em." Even though Sue was only six, she could hold a chicken to the ground.

Jane and I slipped into the coop, closed the door behind us and set about trying to snag roosters. Not hens, just roosters. The coop was a storm of hens and roosters, cackling, flying, dodging. The roosters ran behind the hens, under the roosts, into corners, under and on top of each other, anywhere to avoid us. Chicken feathers along with the acrid smell of chicken manure dust filled the air. I clamped my mouth tight shut, trying not to breathe as I crouched low and duck-waddled as far under the roost as possible, jabbing my wire into the swarming mass of birds, shielding my face against the errant chicken that flew straight at us in a frantic attempt to escape. In such a small space, you would have thought it would be easier.

"Got one," Jane yelped, pulling the wire toward her, grabbing the rooster by its leg and handing it out to Dad.

The competition was on. Ignoring the dust and smell and noise, I forced my way toward the swirling mass of feathers and snagged a rooster of my own. "I got one, too," I crowed.

"Finally," Jane mocked me.

I stuck out my tongue at her and rapidly pulled it back in my mouth. "*Yuck!*" I spit out dust. Jane laughed. I laughed.

"Stop fartin around in there," Dad barked.

We turned our efforts to the roosters.

We either became more skilled in our efforts or the roosters got tired because we succeeded in handing a steady stream of birds out the door.

As Dad took each rooster, he gathered both its legs and the ends of each wing in one hand. Held upside down like this, the bird became quiet. Then Dad laid the rooster, its head extended between two spikes sticking up from a stump, and in one decisive stroke separated head from body.

Even after it loses its head, a chicken has a good deal of nerve energy and will, if let loose, flap its wings and run around just as if it is still alive. This is no doubt where the phrase 'running around like a chicken with its head cut off' comes from. That is one messy way to kill chickens.

To avoid the mess and to avoid having to chase dead chickens all over the yard, Dad handed decapitated birds to Sue. Using both hands, Sue took the chicken from Dad, doing her best to keep the wings and legs contained, as she thrust the chicken's neck to the ground for the few seconds it took until the bird stopped kicking and bleeding.

Growing up on a farm, I never gave a second thought to killing an animal to eat. I don't think any of us did. Chickens, cows and pigs were our livelihood. We raised them, we ate them or we sold them. That was just that.

We could catch chickens and Dad could behead them faster and in greater quantities than Sue could hold, so eventually, either Jane or I—whomever was having less success catching—joined Sue in holding dead birds. It was a point of pride to keep the chicken feathers as clean as possible, so we put the headless birds in the dishpan so their necks all came together in the center, their wrinkly, yellow feet sticking over the edge of the pan. In short order, we had a dishpan full and Mom materialized at our side to cart the dishpan away, leaving an empty pan in its place.

Mom and Grandma Jensen took each dishpan heaped with chickens to the basement where Mom had a pot of water boiling on the gas stove. Taking one chicken in each hand, she dipped the carcasses into the hot water—in-out, in-out, in-out. Three times. Then she tugged at the feathers to test how easily they pulled out of the carcass. Too little time in the hot water and the feathers wouldn't come out. Too long in the hot water and the skin scalded and came off along with the feathers. When each bird was dipped just right, she handed it to Grandma who stripped the feathers off in big handfuls.

Hot, wet chicken feathers stink. When we finished killing chickens—a task done in the clean, open air—and lugged the last dishpan full of dead birds to the basement, we were met by that wet chicken feather smell, an assault to the senses I managed to forget about from year to year. The manure dust in the chicken house was bad; this was worse. "Oh, ick!" I howled, wrinkling my face in disgust.

"Get over here and help." Mom locked me in place with a determined eye as she pulled a chicken out of the pot of hot water and handed it to me. Pulling off feathers was the worst job.

"Ouch, ouch, ouch," I yipped, picking at the tips of scalding feathers with two fingertips.

"Hurry up. You have to pluck those feathers before they get cold," Mom said and dropped two more steaming birds into the pan in front of me.

"It's too hot to touch," I whined.

"Oh, for Pete's sake. You'll never get it done. Give it to me," Grandma said. She took the chicken out of my hands and I watched in amazement as she stripped the bird bare of feathers in less than 30 seconds. It was a known fact that both Mom and Grandma could dip their hands in boiling water and never feel it at all.

"Thanks, Grandma," I smiled and scooted away. "I'll put on some music." A big old console-sized record cabinet that once belonged to my other grandma—Grandma Denter—stood along the basement wall. I opened the lid and blew dust off the turntable before searching out a record. The old Edison was never cranked up and played except when we butchered chickens.

Pawing through the rack of records in the cabinet, I asked, "Which song do we want to hear?"

"*My Grandfather's Clock*," Jane suggested.

"Okay. I'll look for it," I said. Pulling out each heavy black quarter-inch thick disk to read the label, I found other songs we liked, songs like "*O! Dem Golden Slippers*," "*Eleven Cent Cotton*" and "*Where is My Wandering Boy Tonight?*" The records were all the size of LPs but had just one song on each side.

These old songs were a hoot. The scratchy sound of banjos and harmonicas that came out of the console reminded me of black-and-white newsreel footage and the vaudeville shows we sometimes saw on TV. All the songs were sung by men, even the songs where it was a woman's story, like "*I Wish I Was a Single Girl Again.*"

Settling the record on the turntable, I wound the crank on the side of the console until it was tight, released the brake on the turntable, and set the needle carefully at the edge of the record. The sound of a man singing about his grandfather's clock filled the basement.

"Okay, Squirt," Dad said. "Quit fartin' around. Get a knife."

While we had been out killing chickens, Mom and Grandma set up tables, filled tubs of cold water and assembled a stack of sharp knives.

Giving the crank a last turn, I looked at Dad with an innocent smile to confirm I really had not been wasting time, picked up a knife, grabbed a bare naked chicken from the pan of birds Mom had just run through a flame to singe off hair and pinfeathers, and fixed my eyes on Dad's bird.

"Cut the skin by the neck and take out the crop," he said, pointing to the spot on his bird, making a small slit and pulling the gullet out of the chicken's neck. Stationed around the table like a troop of young surgeons, we followed Dad's moves as closely as we could.

"Mine broke," Sue lamented, looking at the mess

created by the nicked crop. Pouring out of the crop was everything the chicken had eaten most recently—corn, oats, bits of sand, grass—all covered in slime.

Leaving off singeing pinfeathers for a moment, Mom stepped in at once. "That's okay," she said. "We can wash that off."

Sliding my bird a few inches further away from Sue's mess, I slipped my fingers through the incision, in under the crop and pulled the lumpy sack out all in one piece. Wiping my hair out of my eyes with the back of my arm, I looked up in triumph. "Got it!"

"Good," Dad said. That was about the extent of approval we could expect from Dad, but that was enough. I grinned.

Without waiting, Dad flipped his chicken around and made cuts in the end 'that goes over the fence last.'

When I'd made the same cuts in my chicken, I took a deep breath before I slid my hand inside the chicken carcass. Staring at the woodpile by the furnace, attempting to think of anything other than having my hand inside a chicken's insides, I worked my fingers along and around the rib cage, loosening the squishy, still warm guts from the sides of the cavity. "Eewww," I wrinkled my nose at Jane when I pulled a handful of blue-green intestines that felt like giant night crawler worms out of the bird. Her mouth a thin, tight line, Jane drew the innards out of her bird. Maybe this was worse than catching birds in the chicken house, worse than plucking stinky, wet feathers.

Before we pushed that mass of guts into a bucket by the table, we separated out the heart, liver and gizzard. His knife suspended in mid-stroke as though he could make our cuts for us, Dad's eyes never left us while we searched for the organs.

"Don't cut that green thing. It'll ruin the meat," Dad said as he watched me remove the liver from my bird. With trepidation, I cut away the little green gall sac. Cutting into the gall sac would release bitter bile and ruin any meat it touched. I loved the liver, so I was extra careful. We never butchered without Dad reminding us of the little green thing.

We each had our favorite chicken part. Mine really was the liver, though I would also fight for the heart. Fortunately we didn't all like the same thing. Jane liked the gizzard. I will grant you that the gizzard presented an interesting butchering challenge but I never wanted to eat one of those hard, rubbery balls. Grandma was the only one to like chicken feet. If Grandma wasn't around when we butchered, chicken feet followed the guts into the bucket. If she was around, Mom boiled up a big pot of chicken feet and Grandma contented herself gnawing on those scrawny bones. I can only assume this interest in chicken feet had something to do with the Great Depression. I never asked her.

When I finished drawing the innards out of my chicken, I gave the bird a satisfied pat and handed him off to Mom. She and Grandma took each carcass and reduced it to parts—wings, legs, thighs, back, breasts—placing each piece into a big washtub of cold water.

Cutting up a chicken took about as long as it took for a record to play all the way through. Between birds, I picked out other records, wound the crank tight again, and reset the needle.

As another gravelly voice blared from the console, we sang along. Since we played the same dozen records every time we butchered chickens, we knew the words by heart. On any other day, we preferred the country & western tunes we heard at the Saturday night wedding dances in town or on the radio while we milked cows. Over the years, we fell in love with Buddy Holly and the Temptations, the Rolling Stones and the Beatles. Our cousin Betty, the first of us to reach high school, taught us to do the Swing. We picked up the Twist on our own. But while we butchered, we sang along to these old songs.

"How do you remember those words?" Mom asked, shaking her head in disbelief and I also think with a bit of dismay. Mom liked the house quiet. Left to her own devices, she never turned on a radio or the TV, preferring to spend time wrapped in her own thoughts.

Dad grinned as we mugged our way through songs like *"Breakfast in My Bed on Sunday Morning"* and *"When Irish Eyes are Smiling."* Dad's smiles caused us to launch into the next song with even greater enthusiasm. For the most part, Dad reserved jokes and laughing for friends and neighbors. So on occasions like butchering, when we could get him laughing with us, we did.

After the first bird, I got over being grossed out by the guts, came to tolerate the smell, and got into seeing how quickly I could finish off each chicken. When there were no more feathers to pluck, no more crops to remove, no more chickens to gut, no more gizzards to clean out or gall sacs to remove, we all turned our knives to cutting up chickens. About that time, Dad generally found a reason to go outside. Following him out of the house was not an option. Not while there were chickens yet to cut up. After Dad left, Mom took over teaching us the fine art of separating chicken leg from chicken thigh, wing from breast, breast from back. At that point, it became a competition to see who could cut up a chicken fastest, who could make the cleanest cuts between bones.

As I worked, I looked over to the corner of the basement where we had housed these very same chickens as baby chicks only a couple of months ago. It was amazing to think how fast they'd grown.

With six people working on the task, we butchered 70 chickens before it was time to start afternoon milking chores. When all the chickens were cut up, Mom released us kids, and she and Grandma handled cleaning up the basement. They also washed the chicken parts a final time, picking over each piece for any overlooked pinfeather before they re-sorted all those mixed-up chicken parts into bags headed for the freezer. By the time they finished, each bag contained all the parts of one whole chicken, so we could have one whole chicken for dinner every Sunday.

"Mmm, smell that chicken," I sighed when we trooped back into the house after church. "When are we going to eat?" Why I asked when we would eat, I don't know. We always ate at noon.

Mom looked up at the clock. "We'll eat at noon," she said, slipping her apron over her dress as she turned on the heat under the kettle of potatoes. "Get busy and set the table. Aunt Joyce's will be here soon."

"Can we change our clothes?" Sue asked, hope in her voice. Why Sue asked if we could change our clothes, I don't know. When we had company, we kept our church clothes on until after we ate.

"No. You can stay dressed up until after we eat. Now don't look at me like that," Mom said when Sue groaned. "Get out the good silverware."

At ten minutes to noon, Mom waved to me, "Go tell the men dinner is on the table."

The men were no more than 15 feet away in the

living room, the same place they would park themselves after we ate—in front of the TV, watching a baseball game. After we ate, however, their snores would echo through the house. *Enough to wake the dead,* Mom would say. *We're just resting our eyes,* they would say. They did love their baseball. And their naps.

Sticking my head in the living room doorway, I yelled at my dad, uncle and cousins, "Come and get it before we throw it to the dogs!" Then I retreated laughing.

At exactly noon, we all sat down at the dinner table, to a big platter of fried chicken, with liver for me, a gizzard for Jane, and 'the part that goes over the fence last' for Dad.

Some things were always the same. Sunday dinner was one of them. And that was good.

A Cow Story

On most days, at around four o'clock in the afternoon, Dad opened the barnyard gate to let the cows in, cows that were standing in the lane, crowding against the gate, mooing. When it rolled around toward milking time, the cows usually came up from the pasture on their own. Their internal clocks and pulsing full udders told them it was milking time.

On other days, though, the cows lingered in the quiet, cool shade of the Back 40. Then Dad stood in the barnyard or in the yard in front of the house, cupped his hands around his mouth, and yelled in a deep voice that carried over the farm's entire 180 acres: "Come boss! Come boss!" Our dog Butch sat by his side, calm but alert to Dad's voice. After calling to the cows, Dad reached down and scratched behind Butch's ears. "Let's see if that does it," he'd say, talking to Butch just as though Butch could understand. Actually I always figured Butch *could* understand because whenever Dad directed him to do something, like go to the house, or round up the cows, or get in the truck, or circle around the pigs, Butch did it.

I often stood by Dad's side, too. I liked being with Dad about as much as anything. When I was with Dad, I got to do important things, learn important things. Those things often had to do with cows.

As Dad waited to see if the cows were making their way back up the lane, he pulled a crumpled, red handkerchief out of his hip pocket, took off the sweat-stained seed corn cap that covered his nearly bald head, and wiped beads of sweat from his deeply tanned face. Usually the cows came to his call. To urge them along, he called again, "Come boss. Come bossy."

On those hot summer days when the cows decided that staying under the trees near the creek was more appealing than the trek back to the barnyard, Dad might look down at Butch and say, "Okay Butch, go get 'em." He would wave his hand toward the pasture and say, "Go get the cows, boy." At Dad's urging, Butch took off like a shot, racing across the barnyard, scooting under fences, taking the most direct route to the pasture, earning his keep as an all-around great cow dog. Very shortly after Butch was gone from sight, we'd see the cows coming up the lane, Butch barking and nipping at their heels, moving them steadily toward the barn. Not running them. Just keeping them moving.

And on other days, for reasons that were never spoken to me, Dad didn't send Butch for the cows but instead would motion me toward the truck. "Come on, Squirt," he'd say. "Let's go get the cows."

Dad gave each of us kids a nickname the day we were born—Tooter, Squirt, Bugs. Mom was not at all happy to have her sweet little girls tagged with such unfeminine labels, but the nicknames stuck. I didn't think much of it until I was a teenager and Dad called me Squirt at a pancake supper in the school cafeteria. I flushed as my classmates laughed and said *Squirt?*, looking at me with big question marks in their voices. It took weeks for them to let it die. Before that embarrassing incident, Squirt was Dad's name for me and I was totally happy to hear him use it. When he called 'Squirt,' I was there, ready to take on whatever chore he threw my way.

One day when Dad said, "Come on, Squirt," we climbed into the old blue Studebaker pickup truck with its worn-smooth, brown leather seats, AM radio that got only one scratchy station, and a coat of dust that smelled of summer, and headed on down the bumpy fence line lane toward the Back 40 pasture. Dad drove with a big right hand on the wheel, his left arm crooked out the open window. With the sleeves of his work shirt rolled up above his elbows every day when he left the house, Dad's forearms tanned a deep red/brown under the summer sun. As we drove, dust as soft and fine as baby powder billowed behind the truck, filtered into the cab and coated the thick hair on his arms, making the dark hairs shimmer faintly gold. The strength in Dad's arms and hands made me feel secure, and when I was older and looking for a husband, strong arms and hands were part of what I looked for.

We drove down the dirt path along the east property line, stirring up more dust. Butch ran ahead. His barking caused the neighbor dog Berle to race to the same fence. The fence ended at the mailboxes where the lane divided to send one branch to our house and one to our neighbor's house, so the dogs could have gone at it for real if they really wanted to. But they didn't. They just ran back and forth for a couple of pointless minutes, barking as though they meant to tear each other to pieces.

The dogs repeated this pseudo fight every single time a vehicle came to either farm, so Butch had worn a path from our house up to the fence and Berle had worn a similar path from the Miller's house to his side of the fence. Butch's path even showed up on the aerial photos taken of our farm over the years. Many things changed about our farm—buildings and fences and crops; but Butch's path to the fence was there as long as he lived. As soon as we passed this section of fence, Butch broke off and ran with the truck.

Dad checked the fences as we passed, noting any that needed repair, and as we drove he told me about the crops, which hay field was ready to cut, how the corn was growing. We had a hammer and a few staples in the truck to make minor fence repairs if needed.

When we reached the Back 40, I hopped out to open the gate. Dad drove through, parked the truck at the top of a hill overlooking the pasture, climbed out and stood leaning against the truck, arms folded across his chest. From this vantage point, he could see from one end of the pasture to the other.

The Back 40 was pasture and timber, never planted to crops. Most farmers in our area had an area they called the Back 40, whether or not it was 40 acres, but in fact ours was about 40 acres along the south end of our farm. A small creek ran the length of the pasture, from the west property line to the east. South of the creek were steep tree-covered hills where we went mushroom hunting in the spring and squirrel hunting in the fall.

I latched the gate and came to stand silent by Dad's side, waiting for him to say what we did next. Many of the cows were still lying in the shade, chewing their cuds, acting for all the world as though they hadn't heard any of the previous calls.

Finally Dad yelled again, "Come, bosses. Get

up there. Come on." This time the edge in his voice was sharper. The cows and we kids knew not to ignore this tone. Reluctantly, the cows got up—they couldn't dally any longer—and headed for the barn. Dad watched them intently. "I don't see 24," he said after some time.

Every cow had a number. Dad could tell them all. He could identify each cow if he could only see its head. He could tell you who she was If he could only see her udder. Over time I came to recognize many of the cows myself—Number 18, the one with the Roman nose; Number 12, the one with the white spot on her side that always made me think of a mountain; Number 6, the one we had to be careful of because she chased us. Dad gave a pleased little smile and nod whenever I pointed out a cow by number, and I swelled with pride. Even though Mom worked with the cows every day, she never knew one from another. She didn't like the cows and she never acknowledged them as individuals. The cows were necessary and it was necessary for her to work with them. She did what was required, but she never enjoyed it.

Number 24 was ready to calve and Dad had been watching her. He wanted cows to calve in the barn where he could help if they needed it. But sometimes a cow calved earlier than he expected, before he got her into a calving stall.

"Where is she? Do you think she's okay?" I looked up at Dad. Number 24 was 'my' cow. Well, she wasn't really my cow, but she was gentle and I liked her best and when she was in the barn, I always gave her a little pat on the side when I walked by.

"Shit," Dad grumbled to himself. I bit my lip to hide a grin. Dad used barnyard swear words as often as he used any other words in his vocabulary. Mom always said,

"*Oh, Harvey,*" with a tone of dismay and reproach that did absolutely no good other than to let us kids know that we were not to swear any time, ever.

The one time I slipped and swore out loud is written in my memory with permanent ink. Lunch box in hand, I was edging across the top of a snowdrift west of the garage, seeing just how far I could get without breaking through the crust. Dad stood watching. Just at that moment I broke through the crust, sinking to my waist in the deep snow.

"Oh, shit," slipped past my lips so quickly, I wondered if I'd actually said it out loud. I looked back at Dad. The look of surprise that flashed across his face let me know he had heard and I waited, not even daring to try to climb out of the hole into which I'd sunk. I waited to be struck dead by the hand of God or just as bad, by Dad's hand.

For what seemed like minutes, I waited. Dad looked at me and then said in a conspiratorial tone only I could hear, "Don't let Ma hear you say that." In that moment, through that one little slip of the tongue, and even though I was only about six years old, I grew closer to Dad and took a step toward adulthood.

Ever after that, I heard Dad swear with a mixture of horror and fascination and a vague awareness of forbidden pleasures. We never spoke of it. I never swore in his hearing again. Still, I understood something new that day.

"She probably went up the hill," Dad said. "If she doesn't come up in the morning, I'll have to come back and find her." Dad scanned the hillside, hoping she hadn't gone far, hoping she would come up with the rest of the herd the next day. But now it was time to milk and he couldn't take time to traipse all over the Back 40.

We climbed back in the truck and I asked, "Can I go along tomorrow? If you have to look for her?"

When he said yes, I almost hoped the cow didn't show up in the morning, so strong was my desire to have an important chore to undertake with Dad.

Cows near to calving like to go off by themselves. Some cows calve easy and they can calve on their own. Some cows calve hard and giving birth could kill the calf and even the cow. Dad didn't want to risk cow or calf.

I was eager to help look for the cow and calf, but Dad didn't always let me. Cows can get protective and it may be dangerous to be around them. Dad wasn't worried for himself but having one of us kids along was just one more thing to worry about. The next morning, I was eager for milking to be over and I didn't let Dad out of my sight in case he forgot he said I could go along. He didn't forget, and finally we were back in the truck headed for the pasture. Jane and Sue came along, too; Jane in the cab taking gate duty; Sue and I in the back.

With the truck bumping over ruts and rocks, Sue and I held tight to the side of its bed to keep from bouncing out, sometimes crouching on bent knees to keep from slamming our tailbones. When Dad stopped the truck by the creek, we piled out.

"We'll start on the west end and work back," he said. "They're usually in this section." We fanned out, moving in a wide swath up the hillside. It was the same pattern we took when we went squirrel hunting. "Keep your eyes open," Dad ordered, as though he thought we thought we were there to play.

The hill was steep and we struggled up the grade, over fallen tree trunks, through blackberry brambles. The air was cool under the trees; it smelled fresh from dew that would not dry until nearly noon. The ground was springy soft under blankets of leaves. Sunlight filtered through the leaf canopy, making cow and calf hard to spot. I wanted to be the one to see them first. I figured it was my right since Number 24 was my cow.

But Sue claimed the honor, calling out, "I see her."

"Stand still," Dad commanded. "We don't want to scare her." We froze in place as Dad walked toward Sue, his footsteps muted on the soft woodland floor.

"There." Sue pointed toward a secluded thicket of fallen tree trunks and young saplings and just like that we could all see the cow. I've seen paintings in which the artist has concealed all manner of faces and figures—horses or wolves or Indians—images that are virtually invisible until someone points them out. It was like that with this cow and calf. The calf was curled up in a nest of leaves, hidden in shadows. If it weren't for the cow's size and movements, we could have missed the calf. The cow stood licking the calf's black-and-white coat, clearing the hair of birth remnants, stimulating her baby's circulation. We must have arrived within minutes of her dropping the calf.

Even as we stood motionless, watching, the mother cow nudged the calf, urging it to stand. The calf pulled its front legs under its body, straightened its back legs, pushing up in an awkward effort to gain its feet. It stumbled as it rose but finally stood upright, tottering. Knowing the goal by instinct and directed along by a gentle nudge from its mama, the calf stumbled toward the cow's udder, nosing around until it latched onto a teat. With neck extended, legs splayed for balance, the calf nursed with vigorous determination. A breeze blew through the trees and the sun flickered off the leaves, shining on the calf's curly hair, damp from the cow's licking. Right then, I wished I was an artist. I would have liked to capture this scene.

As we moved closer, the cow swung its head toward us and lowed softly. Some cows are aggressive after calving, intent on protecting their offspring from threats real or perceived. But Number 24 was gentle. Dad waited a few more minutes while the calf nursed and then stepped closer. He talked to the cow in low tones.

"Good girl," he said, his voice familiar to her from countless sessions in the milk barn. "You did a good job." Running his hands along the cow's side, he noted she had already passed the afterbirth. As he quietly but firmly edged the calf away, he examined it, too. "Looks like we got a heifer," he said, pleasure evident in his voice. He was glad to have a good cow like this one yield a female calf that would grow up and join the herd. "Let's get her down to the truck."

We began the challenging task of getting the calf down the hill. Still wobbly on its feet, the calf stumbled on each step down the steep slope, through the tangle of branches and leaves. The calf bawled at being separated from its mama for even a few minutes. The cow mooed in return and followed us, anxious regarding our intentions for her calf. We helped guide this newest member of the herd with Jane and me keeping our hands on the calf's front shoulders to keep it from falling and Dad pushing, lifting, guiding from behind. Sue scrambled ahead to clear brush out of the way. At the same time we kept a wary eye on the cow lest she make a move to reclaim her baby.

Back at the truck, Dad lowered the end gate, squatted to get one arm around the calf's chest and the other around the calf's rear end. In one swoop he lifted the 80-pound newborn into the back of the truck. Sue and I clambered into the truck bed with the calf, petting its neck and whispering "you're okay, you're okay" to quiet it and to make sure it didn't try to stand up while we drove. Dad latched the end gate, wiped the sweat from his head and neck, and climbed into the cab.

Out of sight of its mama, the calf bawled in earnest as we drove back on the property line lane. The cow came up the barnyard lane. Cow and calf called to each other the entire way like an echo across a canyon except one bawl was young and frantic and scared and the other was deep and anxious and caring.

Back at the barn, Dad herded the calf into one of the pens in the barn where she joined the other calves born this month. The calves were less likely to be injured in the calf pens than if they stayed with the cows, and the cow must take her place in the milking herd in any case. My sisters and I were responsible for the calves, feeding them milk and hay; spreading clean, dry straw for bedding each day; pitching wet straw and manure out of the pens into the wheelbarrow each weekend.

Anytime we came into the barn, the calves rushed to the alleyway, thrust their heads through the slats and bawled, expecting we would feed them. If it was not feeding time, we scratched their heads and let them suck on our fingers, a sensation that was strangely satisfying. At feeding time, we brought pails of milk and let each calf drink its fill. With a new calf like the one we just brought up from the pasture, we had to teach it to drink.

Each new calf was fed the extra-rich colostrum milk from its mother for several days. The thick, yellowish-tinted colostrum transferred the cow's immunity to the calf, ensuring the calf a good start on life. Milk from a cow that just had a calf was kept separate until it returned to its normal white, so calves or cats drank this milk until it cleared.

That night while Dad and Mom milked, I took the galvanized tin pail half full of foamy, warm milk only minutes from the cow and stepped into the pen with the new calf. At 80 pounds, the calf weighed more than I did, but I had experience on my side and commitment to this responsibility. The calf, still unsteady on its feet, bawled with hunger but she had not the least idea how to drink from a pail. Not realizing I carried the answer to her hunger, the calf backed away as I came close. "Come on, baby. You're going to like this," I coaxed, maneuvering until I had the calf wedged between my hip and the side of the pen.

Dipping my fingers in the milk, I clamped my hand over the calf's velvet soft nose so my fingers slipped easily into her mouth. The calf recognized the milk smell and taste and sucked with desperate energy even though she was less than 24 hours old. The texture of sandpaper, her tongue tickled and was remarkably strong. As the calf concentrated on absorbing every last drop of milk from my fingers, I drew her nose down into the pail of warm milk. When she inhaled milk through her nose, she snorted and jerked away. "Wow, that was a surprise, wasn't it?" I laughed, letting her catch her breath before we tried again.

When I dipped my fingers in the milk again, the calf didn't hesitate to suck. Again, I drew her nose down into the milk. This time the calf sucked my fingers and pulled in milk from the pail. She ran out of breath and yanked back again. On the third try, the calf gained a balance between drinking the milk as fast as she could and still breathing. She'd learned to drink from the pail. She might forget again by the next morning, but it usually took just one more experience sucking on my fingers to remember. After that, anytime I came to the barn, whether it was feeding time or not, the calf pushed her head through the fence, jockeyed for position with the other calves and was ready to drink.

Dad watched the first time I taught a calf to drink and then I was on my own. When he filled the calf buckets with milk and sent me off to feed them, he never had to say a word. I knew I could handle the chore and so did he.

Mulberry Pie

We had just floated our bark-and-leaf boats out into the creek that ran through the Back 40 when Sue spotted them.

"Look, Carol. Look at the mulberries!" she yelled, pointing up, down and all around us at the same time.

Overripe berries dotted the ground and were squashed under our feet. Overhead, berries lined the branches, thick and plump and so blue-black we could taste the sweet juice just by looking. Like grasshoppers, we jumped again and again, grabbing the branch tips and pulling them down with one hand as we skimmed the juicy mulberries into our palms and scooped them into our mouths. The saliva of desire formed in the corners of our mouths as we strained to pluck berry after berry, swallowing them almost before we could taste them.

Once we'd stripped the low branches clean, we flopped on the ground, gazing up at the even bigger, even juicier, berries beyond our grasp. So many mulberries!

"I bet we could easy pick enough for Mom to make a pie," Sue said.

Mulberry Pie

"Mmmm. Pie," I hummed. For several moments, we drifted off into thoughts of Mom's pies.

We always had dessert at dinner and supper. Usually pie—that or Mom's special ice water chocolate cake—or ice cream—or ice cream on cake—or ice cream on pie. Always dessert. Often pie.

From time to time when Mom put a pie on the table, Dad would claim that he taught her everything she knew about making pies. While she didn't deny that, we never saw him rolling out the dough that turned into flaky, melt-in-your-mouth crusts.

Rhubarb pie in spring when the green/red stalks shot up with their big floppy, elephant-ear leaves. Peach pie when Dad brought a couple of lugs home from the store for Mom to can. Cherry pie when the Fareway got 20-lb. cans of frozen berries. The occasional, rare gooseberry pie when we happened upon a bush in the pasture with tart green or sweet deep purple berries ready to pick. Mostly apple pies because we had lots of apples and they froze well. Complete, unbaked pies Mom made and stacked up in the freezer ready to pop in the oven over the winter or to take to a funeral or an auction. A lemon pie only once that I remember— Dad didn't like it. Banana cream, chocolate cream, coconut cream pies with toasted, fluffy meringue. Every single time Mom made pie with meringue, she claimed it was watery or pulled away from the crust or was too brown. Every single time, Mom said Edna Hoffman made a better meringue. But I loved how the meringue dissolved in my mouth like sweet air. It was all fine by me.

And mulberry pie, only in the spring. As Sue and I looked up at those branches loaded with berries and sucked the sweet juice off our purple-stained fingers, we figured

43

there just could not be any kind of pie better than mulberry for *today*.

"Pie would be great. If we could find something to stand on, we could do it," I suggested, scrambling to my feet. "And we could make a basket out of one of our shirts." We looked for a fallen tree or rocks or something we could use to boost us a foot higher, but found nothing.

"I know," I said, dropping to my hands and knees. "Stand on my back. See if you can reach the branches."

Stepping gingerly up onto my back, Sue wobbled as she balanced and reached up. With a yelp, she lost her balance, toppled off, rolling into a ball as she tumbled to the ground. "I couldn't reach them anyway," she admitted as we caught our breath laughing.

Suddenly Sue sat up, her brown eyes sparkling with excitement. "I know. We could get a ladder. And if we laid a sheet on the ground, we could shake the tree, all the berries would fall off and we could just roll them into a bucket."

"That would be great," I agreed, jumping to my feet. "We'd have enough berries in 10 minutes. And we can make it a surprise."

Just like that, we took off for the garage. As we raced up the lane, we could already see a fresh pie, hot from the oven, with a big scoop of vanilla ice cream melting on the side.

Getting a ladder was not such an outlandish idea. From time to time, we carried a ladder a hundred yards up to the mulberry tree along the fence by the mailbox. Technically it was Miller's tree, but branches draped over the fence, dangling so many fat black mulberries in front of us each spring that we came home with stained hands, shirts and mouths. The lure of a fresh mulberry pie sent us on that quest at least once a year.

In no time, we'd wrestled the wooden stepladder off the wall of the garage. Sue grabbed one end as I took hold of the other. "It's not so heavy," I said, shifting the ladder from hand to hand to get a comfortable grip. A meticulously folded, clean white sheet sneaked from the linen closet in the hall balanced between us on the edge of the ladder. Empty paint cans we used to collect eggs or pick blackberries hung from our belt loops, ready to be filled with all the mulberries we would collect.

When you're 10 years old and your coconspirator is eight, you don't notice that the trek from the house back to the pasture is close to half a mile over rough ground and mostly downhill.

As we walked, the ladder banged against our bare legs, my arms began to ache, and my fingers grew numb. I shifted the weight from hand to hand. We carried the ladder on our right side; we switched it to our left side. I walked in front; then Sue took the lead. In spite of all of our machinations, by the time we arrived under the tree we had matching red patches on both sides of our legs. And my fingers felt as though they were going to drop off.

"Wow," I huffed a sigh of relief when we dropped the ladder under the tree. "That was heavier than I thought it would be." I rubbed my sore hands down my equally sore legs. "Look," I chortled, "I have black-and-blue marks already!" A visible testament to our adventure.

"Yeah, me, too. But come on. Let's get started," Sue said, fairly hopping around with excitement.

So we did. We tipped the ladder up, positioning it under the most promising looking branches of the tree and spreading the sheet to catch all the berries. Scrambling up the ladder, I shook the limbs. Some berries fell on the sheet; more fell on the ground.

"Wait. I'll move the sheet," Sue said. "We're missing too many." She tugged the sheet here and there, looking back and forth from the branches overhead to the uneven ground below, gauging where berries would fall and roll. "Okay," she stepped back. "Now try."

I shook the limbs again. More berries fell. Some of them hit the sheet; some fell on the sheet but rolled off on the ground; many didn't hit the sheet at all. I came down from the ladder and we gathered up the corners of the sheet to channel the berries into our bucket. Some went in the bucket; some rolled back onto the ground.

We peered into the bucket. Many of the berries were green. How is it that green berries fall off while ripe ones cling stubbornly to the branch? Can you make a pie with green mulberries? we wondered. We didn't know for sure but we didn't think so. Maybe with enough sugar?

This wasn't quite as slick an operation as we'd thought it would be. We stared. All that effort to get a cup of berries.

"But I want a pie." Disappointment filled Sue's voice and her eyes glistened.

"We'll get enough." I tried to convince us both. "We have to keep at it. Come on. Let's move the ladder."

Together we wrestled the ladder under another part of the tree and spread the sheet again. This time Sue climbed up to shake the limbs. Mulberries rained down on the sheet and ground. "It's okay," I said. "We can pick up the ones from the ground."

We fell to our knees picking up berries out of the deep grass. The little piles of berries in the buckets grew though we stepped on just as many. Our fingers, our knees and the soles of our feet resembled the blotchy purple spots blooming on the sheet.

Every couple of minutes we peered into our buckets. Certainly not the bountiful bucketfuls we had dreamed of. When we figured we had enough, we folded up the sheet, collapsed the ladder and began the hike back to the house. Uphill. That old wooden ladder weighed more with every step.

By the time we struggled back to the yard and stowed the ladder in the garage, our hands were scraped red and the sides of our legs were a mottled black-and-blue mess of bruises. But we were back and ready to forget all the hard parts. We had pie in sight.

"Look, Mom! We picked mulberries," Sue exclaimed as we raced into the kitchen, each of us tilting a bucket for Mom to see.

"Oh, girls, these are great. Look how many you have," Mom enthused, as she wiped her hands on her apron and tucked a stray lock of hair behind her ear.

"We think there's enough for a pie," I suggested, the hint totally transparent.

"I believe you're right," Mom said as she glanced at the clock. It was 3:00—still an hour before she had to go out to the barn to start chores. "I'm going to make a pie right now. You sit right here and tell me how you picked all these berries," she urged as she poured glasses of milk and slipped a plate of brownies out of a plastic bag.

"We took the ladder because we couldn't reach them," I said, drawing in a big gulp of milk. Mom opened the flour drawer and measured flour into a mixing bowl.

"Look at my leg," Sue interrupted, flinging her foot up on the edge of the table to display the bruises.

"*Both* my legs," I said, hopping off my chair and dancing in a circle to show off the fabulous black-and-blue marks.

Mom dusted the flour off her hands and touched lightly on the swelling discolorations. She shook her head and tsked, "Those will be big bruises all right. I wondered what you girls were doing when I saw you take the ladder down the lane."

"We brought it back," I said around a mouthful of brownie. Even though it was a long haul, even though it was *really* heavy, it never dawned on us to leave the ladder in the pasture and ask Dad to drive down with the truck to retrieve it. We'd gotten it out; we'd put it back.

"I know you did. I saw that, too. You worked hard for these berries," she said with a smile as she cut lard into the flour.

"We wanted it to be a surprise," Sue added.

"Well, it sure was. You have to tell me every last detail," Mom urged.

So we did. As we talked, Mom rolled out crusts and mixed sugar, flour and butter with the mulberries to make our pie. Never once did she say anything about the white sheet stained purple or the fact that at least half the berries were green. While we sat there telling her all about our adventure, Mom simply made us the sweetest mulberry pie ever.

The Harvest Auction

"Help me, here, Squirt. We need to get a calf ready for the church auction," Dad said as he threw a bale of straw up on the end gate. He cut the twine with his pocketknife and broke up the bale, pushing the sections toward me.

I grabbed squares of clean, yellow oat straw and shook them out, covering every inch of the Studebaker truck bed a foot deep. As I spread straw, Dad fitted panels onto the sides of the truck, creating walls on the truck bed that reached as high as my shoulders.

"There," I said, dusting my hands against my shorts when I finished. "That will be a good bed for the calf to spend the day on." I dropped down on the end gate, dangling my feet over the side, as Dad made sure each of the side panels was tight in place.

"Yup." Dad nodded, giving the last panel a shake. It was solid. "Let's get the calf."

"Why are you going so early?" I asked, trailing him into the barn.

"Gotta get a parking spot under the trees. Don't want the calf to spend all day in the sun."

That made sense. Even though it was the first Saturday of October and days started out cool enough, by afternoon it could get hot. Both parking and shade would be at a premium with all the people that showed up for Salem's annual Harvest Auction.

Dad herded a heifer calf less than six weeks old out of the pen, into the alleyway. "Hand me a currycomb," he said.

I grabbed one of the metal brushes hanging from nails above the cat milk pan and handed it to him. While I traced around the whorl of hair on the calf's forehead with my fingers and admired her blue-black eyes, Dad combed away bits of dirt and manure until the calf's coat was spotless.

"Why a heifer calf? Why not a bull?" I asked. Heifer calves grew into the herd. Giving one away didn't make sense to me; it was giving away the future.

"A heifer is worth more. And a heifer calf out of a good cow like this one was is worth a lot."

"But you always take the bull calves to the sale barn. You get rid of them anyway."

"It's for the church," Dad said.

I recalled a sermon on giving the 'first fruits,' the best you had, to God. Dad was sure doing that.

"Let's get her in the truck. I need to get going."

We nudged the calf out of the barn and Dad scooped her up into the truck bed. The calf nosed around this strange pen for a minute, then knelt down in the bed of straw, her nearly all-white coat shining in the sun.

Dad latched the end gate and climbed into the cab. "Now go help Ma get ready."

I stole one last look at the calf. "Goodbye, pretty girl," I said to her. "See you at church," I yelled as Dad drove off down the lane and I headed to the house. He waved out the window.

In the house, Mom had the kitchen counters and table lined with apple and cherry pies, loaves of homemade bread, and the chocolate chip cookies my sisters and I had made. Mom had baked all week getting ready for the auction. Some pies were sliced and served as part of the meal; the rest went on the bake sale. Jane and Sue were sticking strips of masking tape on each item and writing down prices with a magic marker–25 cents for a loaf of bread, 20 cents for a dozen cookies, $1.00 for a pie.

"Put the cherry pies in there," Mom pointed me to a box lined with newspapers. "We may as well keep them together. Hiram will buy them as soon as we show up." She shook her head as though she could not quite believe this no matter how many times it happened.

Hiram was a painter, a bachelor. He had painted our house and he bought every cherry pie we ever made for any bake sale. After bake sales, he must have eaten nothing else for a week. The way he bought our cherry pies was both funny and a point of pride.

Many women had signature baked goods, special treats made for every church event, bake sale, potluck, goodies sought out by people who came looking for just those specialties. Louise made Blarney Stones—chocolate cake cut into squares, dipped in powdered sugar frosting, rolled in crushed peanuts and then frozen. Stella was known for her fancy cookies–crispy, spritz butter cookies or thumb print cookies topped with jam or date swirls— the kind of cookies other women made only at Christmas. Edna baked wheat bread—Mom's particular favorite—that crumbled when you cut into the loaf. Lucille was famous for her peach pie.

At church functions, I lurked near the food tables, scoping out all the dishes, stomach growling, positioning myself close to the head of the line, waiting for Pastor to lead us in singing grace. Mom guaranteed I would not be so rude as to push in first. But I hovered as close to the front as I could get, keeping my eye on Mom, waiting for her nod to grab a plate and move through the line.

When we had everything ready, Mom handed me a cake carrier that had two levels and held two apple pies. "Put that in the front seat. When we get there, one of you girls run it to the basement and give it to Joanne or Dorothy."

By the time we left the house and drove the six miles to the church, the trunk was full and each of us girls held a box on our lap.

Salem Lutheran Church was a little country church on the edge of Spragueville, a village that claimed fewer than 100 residents. Most in the congregation were farm families like ours.

The church backed up to a field and whether planted to corn or hay or oats, the field was a reminder of our connection to the land. When Mrs. Strohmeyer pulled out the stops on the organ—something she did with gusto and at a volume that blew the sleep out of our brains—and led us through all the verses (Lutherans consider it heresy to skip even one verse) of 'bringing in the sheaves,' I felt a particular connection to God and those fields.

When it came time to hay or pick corn, the men ducked out on Sunday services, leaving the pews lined with women and children. "You gotta make hay while the sun shines," they claimed, a pronouncement accompanied by winks from the men and tsks from their wives.

A place of worship, yes, but Salem was more than that. The congregation was a community gathering to celebrate births, weddings and anniversaries, and to weep when someone died or when someone moved away. Luther League, choir practice, soup suppers, Lenten suppers and worship. We might find ourselves piling into the Chevrolet on any day of the week for some gathering at the church.

During the hot summer months, church activity slowed down. Instead of Sunday school every week, we had a week of Vacation Bible School, which kept us on track to earn our perfect attendance pins. My pin recorded six years of never missing a week, and I wore it with pride.

Before worship on summer Sundays, the ushers propped open the stained glass windows so flies buzzed in and out on breaths of hot, humid air. The men—those who did not have a reason to be out in the fields—abandoned their suit coats and even their ties in favor of open-necked shirts. The heat offered yet another reason for the men to doze during the sermon. I watched as Dad's eyes drooped closed and his head began to nod. Mom waited until his breathing turned to snores before landing a soft elbow poke in his side. From time to time, the sermon was interrupted by the snort of someone startled out of sleep when his head fell forward. Those snorts caused us to giggle, but our giggles were cut short by a glance from Mom.

Paper fans bearing pictures of Jesus with children and lambs graced every pew, tucked under the clips on the backs of the pews where the men hung their hats. I grabbed a fan as soon as we sat down and waved it through the whole service to generate a breeze and to perform a minor act of rebellion. That much physical action by a child during church was frowned upon in any other circumstance. Through the open windows, I could see sun shimmering off the corn tassels and I yearned to slip out to lie on the grass under the trees.

In September, Sunday school classes resumed. Days shortened. Nights cooled. By the time we got to October, things were hopping again. The Harvest Auction signaled the real end of the season.

The event was an all-day affair, and we spent days ahead of that getting ready. The auction drew a crowd from all over. Catholics, Methodists and people from other Lutheran churches threw off theological differences long enough to break bread together and bid at the auction.

The Salem women—divided into the Faith, Hope and Charity Circles—organized and managed the bake sale, the rummage sale and the dinner. People bought tickets for the meal. A dollar and a half bought a meal that included roast beef with mashed potatoes and gravy, corn, homemade rolls, red or green or yellow or orange Jell-o salad dressed up with cans of fruit salad or bananas or marshmallows or oranges or raspberries or combinations of any of those. It is believed that church ladies can make Jell-o salad in more variations than there are stars in the sky. And, of course, pie for dessert.

While the women busied themselves with the dinner, the bake sale and the rummage sale, the Salem men organized the auction. They stacked smaller items on hayracks that abounded with household goods—silverware, pots and pans, aluminum perk coffee pots, crocheted doilies, hand towels, outgrown toys, dolls, stuffed animals. Hayrack items were auctioned first, followed by tools—spades and shovels, rakes and hoes, hammers and screwdrivers. More valuable items ringed the edges of the parking lot. If you needed something–and even if you didn't need it–you could find it at the auction. Beneath the shade trees were items that earned the Harvest Auction its name—bushels of apples and potatoes, bags of onions and carrots, a cooler full of frozen containers of blackcaps and blackberries, crates of multicolored Banty chickens, gunny sacks full of walnuts, single bales of straw and hay representing the truckloads farmers donated, pigs big enough to butcher, and our calf—the fruits of a farming community.

When we pulled into the churchyard, the lot was filling up. I looked for Dad.

"I don't see the truck. Dad should be here by now, shouldn't he?" I turned to Mom.

"He'll be along." Mom spoke without taking her eyes off the route she was navigating across the lawn to get near the schoolhouse door. "Let's get these things inside."

As we unloaded boxes, it looked as though we could stock the bake sale all on our own, but when I walked inside the school, it was clear every other woman had been equally busy.

"What do you have there, Carol?" Miss Barr peered into the box cradled in my arms.

"Cherry pies." I smiled up at my Sunday school teacher, a tall, slender woman with perfectly styled red hair. Miss Barr organized the bake sale. And the Sunday school. And Vacation Bible School. Miss Barr was as reliable and meticulous in organizing events as she was in styling her hair. Nothing out of place. Ever.

Thank goodness she was occupied organizing the bake sale. Otherwise for sure she'd ask me if I had Psalm 23 memorized yet.

I squirmed, remembering Vacation Bible School and the debacle of my recitation. Normally I could memorize anything, easy. I had worked on this Psalm, saying the verses over and over to myself and out loud. I had it, I was sure of it. When it came time to recite, I stood and spoke with assurance all the way to the end: "Though annointest my head with oil. My cup runneth over." I sat down.

"Shirley ..." Miss Barr said.

I looked at Shirley Kemp, a younger girl with thin blond hair, sitting next to me. Her turn.

Shirley stared back at me.

"Shirley ..." Miss Barr nodded at me.

I stared at Shirley and then at Miss Barr. Why was everyone looking at me?

"Shirley, goodness ..." Miss Barr nodded at me again.

At that moment it dawned on me that Miss Barr meant for me to continue. That she wasn't saying Shirley; rather she was saying *Surely*. Of course there was another verse. Still seated, I blurted out the words I knew so well, "Surely goodness and mercy shall follow me all the days of my life," I gulped a breath, "and I will dwell in the house of the Lord forever."

Everyone laughed. I blushed, tucked my hands under my legs, stared at my shoes and tried to disappear.

"That's good," Miss Barr said. "We'll do it again tomorrow."

As I stood there holding the box of pies, I hoped Miss Barr had forgotten that whole episode.

"Mmmm," Miss Barr said. "Those smell as good as they look. Laurel has desserts on that table." She pointed toward a woman arranging a long table already filling up with pies and cakes and cookies and bars. "Just give them to Laurel ..."

"I've been waiting for you!" a man's voice boomed.

I looked over my shoulder and saw the familiar white painter's pants. I'd never seen Hiram wear anything else, even when he wasn't working on a job. "Hi," I mumbled, suddenly bashful. "Mom said you might want these."

"Sure do. These are the best cherry pies." Hiram pulled his wallet out of his pants pocket and turned to Miss Barr. "How much do you need for these? I can put them right in my car and they'll be out of your way."

"One dollar each," Miss Barr looked straight at Hiram, her voice firm, as though she half expected him to object to such a price.

"Sold!" Hiram exclaimed, commandeering the three pies still warm from our oven. "Worth every penny."

Doug stuck his head in the schoolhouse doorway and caught my eye. "We're having a race. Bet you can't beat me."

"I'm coming," I said, looking at Mom who nodded.

"We've got it all. Go on." She was already heading toward the table in search of Edna's wheat bread.

I raced off after Doug. A year younger than I, Doug ran everywhere and though I seldom beat him, I never stopped trying.

The churchyard was swarming with kids and we all knew each other well. We went to church so often, all these kids were almost like brothers and sisters. The other parents were just like so many added sets of parents. And none of those adults hesitated to set us back in line if we stepped off track—particularly when it came to running or yelling in the sanctuary.

While we'd been carrying things inside, Dad had arrived. I didn't see Dad anywhere, but I headed to the pickup, with Doug in tow. "Come see our calf," I urged. "It's a heifer. I helped Dad get her ready."

We scrambled up on the truck bumper and clung to the panels, looking down into the truck bed.

"Nice calf," Doug agreed.

I nodded, but I was confused. This was not the calf I helped Dad load up. That calf was mostly white. This calf was mostly black. In addition, this calf wore a halter and was tied on a short rope. I looked around for Dad but didn't see him anywhere.

"Let's go," Doug jumped down from the truck and ran toward the church. "It's time to eat."

I looked at the calf again. Why would Dad bring a different calf from the one we loaded?

"Come on," Doug shouted.

Jumping down, I tore off after Doug. Dinner was most important. I would ask Dad about the calf later.

With a full stomach, including a Blarney Stone and a slice of banana cream pie, I wandered out of the church basement and into a yard full of cars and people milling around, checking out the auction goods. I spotted Dad standing in the shade of a pine tree, smoking a cigarette, talking with some men. As I walked up, I overheard him say, *If I'd tied her down, it wouldn't have happened.* When Dad saw me, he stopped talking, dropped the cigarette to the ground and stubbed it out with his toe.

I tugged on his sleeve. "Dad."

"What?"

"Our calf. Doug and I looked in the truck. It's not the same one we loaded this morning."

Dad looked at the other men.

"How's your corn looking?" one of them said as he dropped back a step.

"Good," the other replied. "We'll be picking soon," They faded away leaving Dad with me.

"It's not the same calf," I repeated.

Dad looked at me for quiet seconds and in those seconds a little chill ran up my back.

"No. No, it's not the same calf."

"Well, where is she?"

"I had to get another calf."

"But, why? You said the one we had was one of the best."

"She was." Dad crouched down on his heels and looked me straight in the eyes. "On the way in, she tried to jump out of the truck." Dad hesitated. "When she tried to jump out, she fell and broke her leg."

My stomach went hollow. "Will she be all right? Where is she? Can I see her?"

"No, Squirt. I had to put her down."

Tears welled in my eyes. I felt my throat clench and my face go red as I struggled against crying. It was not as though this calf was more special to me than any other calf. But I had helped get her ready. And she was the best.

Dad put his hand on my shoulder and the warmth sank into my skin. The tension drained out of my face.

"Let's go now," he said. "We don't want to miss the bidding. Shorty told me he's going to start with that stray dog."

Dad did not linger on the calf he lost nor would he let me. Together, we walked over to the hayrack where someone lifted up a puppy that looked as though its parents included Beagles, German Shepherds, a Collie and any range of mutts. It was very cute.

"We're going to start the auction with this little puppy," Shorty called out to the crowd. "She needs a good home and we hope to find her one. Who'll start the bidding at a dollar?" Someone raised a hand. "*All right, got one-let'sheartwo-two-gottwo-howaboutthree.*" The auction was off and running.

Shorty was a farmer, a professional auctioneer and he also sang with a band at wedding dances on Saturday nights. He and Johnny called the Harvest Auction every year. They knew how to work a crowd, helping novice bidders get into the game and encouraging experienced bidders to go higher.

When the puppy sold, the winning bidder donated the puppy back. That little puppy was sold and donated back at least four times during the day until she went home with the people who bought her the first time.

I slipped in and out of the bidding crowd during the afternoon. But when everyone stood in front of our truck and Shorty drew the crowd's attention to our calf, I wiggled through to stand at Dad's side. "This is one of Harvey's best heifer calves," Shorty said. "You won't find a better calf in these parts. Let's start this one out at $25."

I gasped. I looked at Dad. He was holding back a smile.

25overherenow35-35-35-now40got40now50-50-50got50-50-60-70got80allright

The bidding was fast and furious and it took several moments for me to realize Dad was bidding, too. On his own calf! Shorty's eyes darted back and forth, catching and signaling bids with his hands and urging the bidders on. Looking around, I saw that several men were watching Dad as much as they were watching Shorty. Each time Dad bid, one of them would bid, signaling in the almost invisible way of experienced auction goers: a wink, a nod, a raised finger. Motions the casual observer would never even see. The bidding on our calf was a game, just like selling the dog, and they were all in on it.

Got85-85-85let'skeephergoingboysthiscalf'llmakeagoo dcowgot85-90-90

A cheer went up from the crowd. The bids came more slowly as the price crept up, but Shorty urged the crowd on.

Don'tstopnowboys90-90howabout92-92-got92-92- now95-95-95. It looked as though the bidding might be over when Shorty caught a bid from Dad.

now100

Another cheer from the crowd.

100-100- Shorty scanned the crowd, taking in every man who had bid up to now. None of the other bidders raised a hand, dipped a head or winked.

100 going once . . . going twice . . . going three times. Sold! For one-hundred dollars to Harvey Denter!

The crowd cheered and clapped and laughed. It was the most paid for any one thing at the auction so far.

Dad bought back his own calf. For $100. I didn't know much but I did know that $100 was a *lot* of money.

"You'll get flies in your mouth," Dad said when he saw me gaping at him. I pulled my mouth shut but incomprehension clogged my mind. "I couldn't let that good calf go," he confessed.

Dad had donated two calves and then bought the donation back. This was a twist on giving, a level of sacrifice, that was beyond my understanding. I ran off to tell Mom.

"He did?" Her eyebrows arched and she shook her head one-quarter inch. "Well, it's for the church."

Turning 10

The Big Ben alarm clock erupted, clanging in the predawn quiet like a spoon on the sides of an empty soup pan. The silver-green, glow-in-the-dark hands pointed to 5:15. I fumbled to shut it off even as I struggled to pry open my eyes.

Flinging off the blankets, I swung my legs over the side of the bed and sat up. I was afraid if I closed my eyes for even a few seconds, I'd be asleep again. I'd lain awake last night thinking about this day, as excited as if the dawn would bring Christmas morning.

Next to me in bed, Sue burrowed down under the covers, cocooned in the warm nest I had just vacated, blissfully unaffected by the alarm. At eight years old, my younger sister would not get up until 6:30. Until yesterday, I'd slept in just like she did. But yesterday I turned 10.

As I pulled on my pants and sweatshirt, I heard Jane fumbling around in her room down the hall. In the dark, we sat on the mud room steps and struggled to pull stubborn rubber galoshes over our shoes before we headed out the

63

door. The first light of dawn was breaking and dew was heavy on the grass as we trekked down the hill to the barn.

Jane saw me yawn and gave me a light jab in the arm. "Get used to it," she laughed.

Stifling another yawn, I grinned back at her and took a deep breath of cool October air that made my lungs and skin tingle. Reaching up over my head, I cupped my hands around the Morning Star as if it could hold my excitement over how grown up I felt to be heading for the barn to help milk the cows.

Each morning, Dad left the house at 4 a.m., way before it got light out, to start the milking chores. Every morning and every evening of every single day of the year he milked cows. Start to finish, the milking chores took about three hours, though the actual milking of the 50 cows only took an hour or so. When Dad went to the barn, he set the milking machines together, poured a bucket of grain in front of each stanchion, and opened the barn door for the cows to file in.

Just like chickens, cows have a pecking order so when Dad opened the barn door he knew which cows would come in first. The same 10 cows came in the first batch, the same 10 came in the second batch, and each cow always went to the same stanchion.

Milking began exactly at 5 a.m. Dad was particular in that way, as precise as his German ancestors. Mom was supposed to get up after Dad did, but sometimes she fell back to sleep and then his impatient voice at the door jolted all of us out of sleep: "Ma! It's time to milk!" When Dad had to trek back to the house to wake Mom up, he wasn't happy. At the sound of his gruff voice, Mom scrambled out of bed and hurried to the barn where she took over washing the cows' udders with warm iodine water and attaching the milking machines.

When a cow finished milking, Dad took the milking bucket off the cow and emptied the warm, foamy milk into five-gallon pails. This is where Jane came in. It was her job to carry those heavy pails into the milk house and pour the milk into the bulk tank.

With time and strength, one person could milk the cows. But more hands made a difference. When any one of us wasn't there, someone else had to carry that weight.

Nearly 12 years old, Jane had been carrying milk for a year and a half. Since she turned 10. Now I had reached that milestone and it was my turn, too.

Before I turned 10, my barn chores included feeding the calves during the evening milking and bedding their pens with fresh straw after school each day. It may sound crazy, but I aspired to carry milk, and I was more excited about getting to do that than to open any present I found on my breakfast plate that year.

On my birthday, Mom made our traditional birthday cake to celebrate—a white layer cake with chocolate pudding between the layers and fluffy white, seven-minute frosting mounded in dramatic swirls on the top and around the sides. Ten candles burned as she carried it to the table at noon and everyone sang. I looked at Dad. I looked at the candles. I wished and wished as I blew them out. Dad didn't disappoint me.

"You come to the barn with Jane in the morning," was all he said. I didn't even try to hide my grin.

When Jane and I unlatched the barn door that morning and stepped into the alleyway by the calf pens, it was like I was seeing the barn and the cows and all the action for the first time, seeing it with a mind full of desire for grown-up responsibility.

"Morning, babies," I murmured to the calves that stuck their heads through the slats and started bawling as soon as they saw us. I stopped to scratch the black-and-white hair that curled in tight whorls on their foreheads. Cats waiting for milk wound figure eights around my legs.

The barn pulsed with quiet rhythms during milking. The cows wiped up every kernel of grain from the manger with their long tongues and then stood placidly chewing their cuds, lowing occasionally in response to calves bawling in the nearby pens. Light from bare bulbs and the even, heartbeat thumping of the vacuum pipe that ran the milking machines suffused the barn. Up on a ledge, a dust-covered radio fed us a steady stream of weather and farm reports, local news and country music.

"Squirt, Tooter, get the buckets. You can feed the calves with this milk," Dad said when he saw us. We grabbed the galvanized pails from the hooks in the alley and set them down by the feedbox just as Dad pulled the teat cups off a cow, flipped off the vacuum valve, disconnected the hoses, and lifted the heavy milk bucket off the belt hanging around the cow's middle.

When he poured a measure of milk into each of the calf pails, I saw that the milk was tinged yellow. That cow had calved recently and I knew her milk couldn't go in the tank yet. "Tooter, make sure the new calf gets some of this," Dad said. Jane nodded. We picked up the buckets and Jane stepped into the calf pen to feed the newest baby calf while I stayed in the alley and fed other calves through the slats.

The oldest and strongest calves shoved the smaller ones out of the way, plunging their noses deep into the fresh, warm milk. "Hey. Don't be so pushy. You'll all get some," I growled. Struggling to hold the pails steady, I wedged them against the side of the pen, bracing each one with a knee. With the weight off, I could flex my fingers and get the blood flowing again. Dad could balance two buckets in each hand and feed four calves at the same time. I would do that, too, someday. Today, just two buckets presented a challenge.

It took only seconds for the calves to drain the buckets. After the calves sucked up all the milk they could, I tipped the remaining drops into the cat pan where half a dozen cats waited to lap it up. This was the kind of work I already did during evening milking. Carrying milk was the new challenge.

With the calves fed, Jane and I stepped up by the five-gallon pails, ready to take over carrying milk, a task Dad and Mom had handled before we got to the barn.

"Tooter, you help Squirt," Dad said.

"I know how," I protested.

"The bucket's heavy. It'll take both of you," Dad said and he filled the pail nearly to the brim.

Positioning ourselves on either side of the pail, Jane and I lifted at the same time. Taking short steps, struggling not to spill even a drop, we made our way with the heavy pail to the milk house. As Jane pushed open the milk house door, I heard Mom say, "Harvey, they can't lift that." Glancing over my shoulder before the door swung shut behind me, I saw Dad watching us. "Hmmph," he grunted as he crouched down between two cows. I was going to prove that I could lift the pail. I could do the job.

"Wow," I whistled once Jane and I were in the milk house and set the bucket down. "This is heavy." We flexed our fingers. I stared up at the strainer on top of the bulk tank. I looked down at the pail full of milk. Forty pounds at least. Maybe 50. "How are we going to get it up there? It's so high."

The bulk tank filled half of the milk house. A stainless steel monster, the tank was big enough to hold the milk from milking the cows morning and night. A cooling system at one end of the tank ran a paddle that stirred the milk and cooled it as we poured more in.

The top of the bulk tank met me at eye level. The stainless steel strainer, fitted with a disposable filter pad, was positioned in a porthole on top of the tank.

"We can do it," Jane said. "We both have to lift at the same time."

"I don't know," I eyed the bucket and the strainer warily.

"We can. Grab hold," Jane ordered. "Are you ready?" she asked when I'd taken a position opposite her and had a good hold on the pail handle.

I nodded.

"When we get it halfway up, rest the pail on your knee, grab the bottom of the bucket with one hand and we'll lift it the rest of the way."

I drew a big breath and held it as we lifted the bucket and balanced it first on a knee and then lifted again to lean it against the edge of the strainer. When we rested the weight of the bucket against the strainer, the strainer tilted. Milk splashed. "Yipes!" I jerked as milk soaked through my sleeve.

"Hold it still," Jane barked.

"I'm trying," I gasped through gritted teeth as we righted the bucket. "It's heavy."

"Okay. Lift again. Tip the pail just a little." We lifted the bottom of the bucket higher and poured the milk a little at a time into the strainer. Jane was two inches taller and I strained on tiptoe to keep my side of the pail even with hers.

"Not too fast. It'll run over," she said.

When we finally emptied the last milk into the strainer, I breathed a sigh of relief and stared at Jane. "How do you lift that by yourself?"

She shook her head, "Dad doesn't usually fill the buckets that full. I guess he thought we could do it."

"I can't." I shook my head. Here I'd been given a chance to help with the milking and it was clear I wasn't going to be able to. The excitement I'd felt earlier drained out. Instead, fear that I could not do the job knotted my stomach.

"You'll get the hang of it. Come on. We have to get going." Jane grabbed the empty pail and I trailed behind her back into the barn. I was not so sure.

When we set the bucket down in the alleyway near the cow Dad was milking, neither Jane nor I said anything about splashing the milk. But looking up at us as he squatted between the cows, Dad's eyes trailed over the milk-soaked sleeve plastered clammy and cold to my arm. "Squirt, go get another pail out of the milk house." I ran back into the milk house and grabbed the nearest pail off the rack on the wall.

When Dad took the bucket off the next cow, he poured half the milk into Jane's pail and half into mine. I hoisted the bucket alone. I took a few steps, wobbling under the weight, the edge of the pail scraping against the side of my leg. It was still heavy. Straightening my back, I kept walking. If Jane could do this, so could I.

Jane leaned her back against the milk house door and pushed through. I did the same. Once inside, we set our buckets down. "Look at my hand," I said, showing her the white ridges where the pail handle pressed into my fingers.

"Yeah. Me, too," she said in a matter-of-fact tone, turning her palms up to me. "You get used to it. Come on. I'll help you empty your pail."

When we lifted the half-full pail of milk between us, it felt light by comparison. This time, we didn't spill any.

"Let me show you how to do it yourself," she said after we emptied my pail. In one swift move, she took the other pail of milk, lifted it with both hands until she could rest the bottom rim on her knee. Then she held the handle with one hand and grabbed the bottom rim of the pail with the other. With what looked to me like superhuman strength and in one even move, she lifted the pail up until the top edge rested lightly against the strainer. She emptied it without spilling a drop. "Got it?" she asked when she brought the pail down from the strainer.

"I think so." I frowned. "What if I spill it?"

"You won't. Now let's go," she said and turned back to the barn.

I grabbed the other pail and followed. I hoped I wouldn't. I wasn't so sure. My confidence was not as great as when we walked down the hill from the house. This was a lot harder than I had thought.

I set my empty milk pail near the cow Dad would finish milking next. He was crouched down by the cow, checking the flow of milk from the teat cups into the milking machine. Just as he looked up at me, the cow swished her tail and smacked him flat across the face. I clapped a hand across my mouth to stifle a giggle. Dad grimaced, grabbed the cow's tail and tucked the end behind his bent knee. "That'll fix her," he said, winking at me.

Dad moved among the cows with confidence. Meanwhile, Mom was tentative, wearing a hesitancy she telegraphed to me in a tight smile and to the cows in her abrupt movements.

Carrying a small bucket of water, Mom squatted down between the cows, washing each udder clean of manure and dirt. When the udder was clean, she tugged on each teat, squeezing out a squirt or two of milk. Those squirts of milk cleaned out the duct and encouraged the cow to let down her milk. That task accomplished, Mom took one of the milking machines, hooked the hose to the vacuum line and attached a teat cup to each teat. Then she moved down the line, stepped between the next two cows and crouched down to do it all again. Mom did these tasks morning and night, every day of the year. But she never came to like it.

Thinking about it for more than two seconds, you will understand why Mom was never quite at ease. While washing udders, Mom put her 140 pounds between two cows with a combined weight of more than a ton. If two cows decided for any reason to step toward each other at the same time, anyone standing between them absorbed a ton of pressure. Literally. Dad's ribs were cracked more than once.

Cracked ribs were rare. More likely, you'd get a manure-caked tail swished in your face, a slap made worse when it was raining and the manure in the barnyard turned to a slurry despite Dad's efforts to keep the yard clean. Plus, some cows were kickers, frightened or annoyed or just testy about anyone touching their udders. Dad handled these problems by keeping his forearm in contact with the cow's leg both to ward off a kick and to let her know he was still there. Steady and calm himself, Dad kept the cows steady and calm. The cows made Mom nervous, but she never gave up.

Before there was time for the white ridges to recede from my hands, Dad emptied another milk bucket, dividing the milk evenly into our pails. We lugged these much more manageable pails into the milk house. This time, Jane let me go first.

Determined to do it just right, just like Jane did it, I clenched the handle with both hands, lifted the pail of milk until the bottom edge rested on my knee and the rim of the bucket leaned against the side of the tank. I looked at Jane and she nodded. I repositioned one hand under the bottom of the bucket, took a deep breath and lifted the pail up over my head so the bucket now balanced precariously on the edge of the strainer. My arms quivered and for a terrified second I had visions of spilling all the milk on the floor.

Fear can make you ever so strong. I tightened my puny arm muscles and forced the pail to remain steady as I poured milk into the strainer. It was only when I brought the pail down and set it on the floor that I realized I'd been holding my breath. I gulped in air as I wiped sweat off my forehead with the hem of my shirt.

"Good job." Jane smiled. "You did it."

I had done it. That felt good. But then, lest I get to feeling too proud of my effort, Jane whipped her pail up to the strainer and emptied it as though it weighed nothing. I gazed at her with nothing short of adoration. Back to the barn we went and I put my pail down near Dad.

As I stood there, out of the corner of my eye, I saw a cow down the row arch its back, a signal it was going to pee. I grabbed my pail and took a quick, giant step backwards to avoid the splatter. In the course of milking, you just couldn't avoid getting cow pee or poop on yourself. But at least I could do my best to keep it out of the milk pail. When the cow finished, I moved my pail back up close so Dad didn't have to carry the milker very far.

Dad filled our pails. We emptied them. Back and forth we went, carrying pail after pail to the milk house. If a cow didn't give a lot of milk, there might only be enough milk for one of us. Those times, Jane and I traded off carrying. With each pail emptied into the tank, my confidence returned.

"Okay?" Jane caught my eye when I returned from a solo run.

"Did it." I beamed. "Easy."

She raised an eyebrow. "Easy?"

"Easy."

Jane handed me her pail. "Then you can take both pails," she said. "I'm going to go bed the pens."

My mouth dropped open. "Wha …?"

"Carrying two is easier than carrying one," she explained. "You're more balanced."

Before I could protest, she was gone. I turned a questioning eye toward Dad. He nodded and divided the latest bucket into the two pails. "She's right," he said.

Okay, if he thought I could do it, I thought I could do it. I grabbed the handles and lifted. The muscles in my shoulders knotted and the handles dug deep grooves in my fingers as I struggled to walk to the milk house, the rims of the buckets chafing against the sides of my legs. At the milk house door, I turned my back and pushed in. By the time I set the pails back down, my arms were quivering. I shook my arms, curling and uncurling my fingers. I stared up at the strainer.

"Okay," I muttered. "Here we go." Grabbing the first

pail with both hands, I brought it up to my knee, shifted one hand to the bottom of the pail and lifted it up to the strainer. The milk surged, filling the strainer to the top. I eased the pail back, let the milk drain down, and poured the rest in.

"Easy," I said when I set the pail on the floor. "I can do this." The other pail wasn't even half full. No problem. I don't want to say I got cocky, but maybe just a little overconfident.

Smug in my success emptying the first pail, I grabbed the second bucket and swung it up with one hand instead of lifting with both hands like Jane taught me. Without repositioning my hands, I shoved the pail straight up to the strainer. In my enthusiasm, the pail went too high, too fast. The stainless steel pail crashed against the strainer with a resounding clank, the strainer tilted haphazardly to one side.

In a split second, everything switched to slow motion. The milk splashed high and wide, and I watched in horror as that precious liquid streamed down the side of the tank, formed a white river across the floor and disappeared down the drain.

Frantic, I struggled to get both strainer and bucket back to level. Seconds felt like hours as I righted the strainer and finished dumping what little milk remained from the pail into the strainer. With the pail emptied, I grabbed the hose to wash away all traces of the spilt milk, all the while praying no one would come in to witness this disaster.

When I had everything cleaned up, I snatched the buckets and hurried back to the barn, casting one last glance behind me to be sure all the milk was gone from the sides of the tank and washed down the drain.

When I set the pails down near Dad, I could not

meet his eyes. If he just looked at me, I was sure he could see what I had done. Humbled by my foolish haste, I knew I would not be so careless again.

But the milk house was a separate world from the barn. While I'd been cleaning up my spilt milk, another problem revealed itself with a cow.

"I think this one might have mastitis," Mom told Dad as she finished washing a cow. The milk she squirted out of one cow's teat came out clotty thick like sour milk. Mom would not put the milker on until Dad checked it out.

When Mom stepped away, Dad planted his hand firmly on the cow's haunch, stepped in and crouched down to check her out. He squeezed milk from all four teats. Three of them were fine, but sure enough, milk from the fourth teat continued to be clotted even after several tugs.

"Shit," he muttered.

Mom sighed a reproach. If Dad heard her, he gave no sign.

"Okay, we'll milk her out and use the milk to feed the rest of the calves," he said. "Squirt, get a tube out of the box."

I ran to the small wooden medicine box on the wall by the feed box, lifted the lid and picked out one of the mastitis treatment tubes.

"This?" I asked, holding the tube up to show him before I closed the lid. Dad nodded and stuck the syringe in his shirt pocket so it would be handy as soon as he took off the milker.

Once he milked the cow out and poured all the milk in the calf buckets, Dad inserted the large, plastic syringe into the inflamed teat and injected the full dose of antibiotic. Milk from this cow could not be sold until the mastitis cleared up and the antibiotic cleared her system.

I'd watched the milk hauler take a sample of milk from the tank and store it in the cab of his truck before he siphoned the milk from our tank into his truck. Samples taken every day from every farm on the trucker's route were taken to the milk plant. Before the truck was unloaded, the plant tested a sample of milk from the tanker. If that sample showed any antibiotic trace, all the milk in the truck was dumped. Then each farm's sample was tested. The farmer who let milk from a treated cow get into the tank was charged for the lost cost of the whole load. Dad never made a mistake.

Cow by cow, Dad and Mom worked their way down the rows, washing an udder, putting on the belt, attaching a milker, washing the next cow, putting on the belt, attaching a milker, checking how the first cow was doing, washing another udder, putting on the belt, attaching a milker, checking the second cow, taking the milker off the first cow, emptying the bucket, attaching it to the third cow, checking the second cow, and on and on. And Jane and I carried the milk of every cow and dumped it into the tank. There is a routine to milking cows, a constancy like the rising and setting sun, that is both comfortable and comforting.

In an hour we worked our way through milking all fifty cows in the herd. "I'm going to the house to start breakfast," Mom said the moment she attached a milker to the last cow. She left the barn barely acknowledging Dad's comment that we'd be up to the house within the hour.

Dad moved on to check another cow's progress. The milking was almost done but chores weren't.

When the milking machine came off the last cow, Dad walked down the line, releasing the stanchions, slapping each cow on the shoulder to get her to back up. "Get out of here now," he ordered. The cows complied, contented now that their udders were empty to amble out to the hay bunk in the barnyard.

As soon as the last cow was out the door, I grabbed a broom and swept down the stalls and alleyways; Jane shoveled manure out of the gutters. Dad climbed up to the haymow and threw down a couple of bales to feed the calves. After breakfast, Mom would come back to the milk house to wash the milkers and buckets.

"That looks like it," Dad said when we finished the barn chores. Sleep long gone from my mind, I stood surveying the barn, feeling strong, imminently useful, and more than a little hungry. Standing beside Dad, my fear that I could not do the work was gone. I'd spilled milk but I wouldn't do that again. I hoped.

I slipped my hand still bearing the ridges imprinted by the bucket handles into Dad's big strong hand. He gave me a squeeze, rested his other hand on Jane's shoulder, and we walked up the hill to breakfast.

There was nothing magic that happened to me between the last day I was nine years old and the day I turned 10; I was still a kid. Of course, I could not do the work of an adult at that age. But the work I did, the work all three of us kids did, had meaning. Everything we took on lessened the load Dad and Mom carried. Everything they asked us to do increased our sense of value to ourselves and to our family and to the farm. And because Dad and Mom valued what I did, that was the best gift of all.

House Chores

"What are we having for breakfast?" Mom asked with studied casualness as we finished putting away the supper dishes. Her question was a combination reminder that I was cooking—as if I could forget that; a check on the completeness of the menu—it was pretty much a given that in my inexperience I'd forget something; and a chance to offer help if I needed it without ever actually coming out and saying *Do you need help?*, which would have made me feel inadequate when I was trying hard not to be.

"Pancakes and sausage, I think," I said, glancing up quickly to see if she agreed with my choice. I slipped pancakes into the meal rotation as often as I could when I was cooking. They were my favorite breakfast ever since I was a little kid and Mom set me on top of the freezer next to the gas stove in the basement to watch as she poured pancakes in the shapes of elephants and rabbits and the occasional and infinitely more difficult giraffe on the big round cast-iron griddle. In addition to liking them, pancakes were one of the few things I felt confident making all on my own.

79

She nodded. "You'll need to get a package of sausage out of the freezer tonight, then." When I nodded and headed toward the cellar, she added, "Better check and see if there's enough tomato juice in the refrigerator."

As though it had been my plan all along, I changed course to scope out the juice supply. "At least a quart. Looks like enough to me," I said, bounding off to the basement.

"It's in the basket on the left," she called, anticipating my next challenge before I'd had a chance to think of it.

A blast of cold air hit my face as I lifted the heavy lid to the chest freezer. The one-pound packages of pork sausage, tightly wrapped in white freezer paper, stamped in blue ink to identify the contents, were indeed piled in a wire basket on the left. Looking at the neatly stacked packages of meat, Tupperware boxes of vegetables, and apple and rhubarb pies ready to bake, I wondered if she had the location of every item in the freezer memorized. It wouldn't have surprised me. Grabbing a package of sausage, I let the freezer lid drop shut. I was glad the sausage was on top. Sometimes I had to pull a chair over to the freezer and practically stand on my head to reach certain items.

Running, I took the cellar steps two at a time and dropped the sausage brick into the kitchen sink. It would thaw by morning.

The next morning, after feeding the calves, I raced up the hill to the house. Leaving my boots and coat on the porch, leaping the three steps into the kitchen, I felt a tiny wave of pride sweep through me. And trepidation. Cooking breakfast. By myself.

Shortly after my 10th birthday, about the same time I got to start carrying milk, Mom got it in her head I was also old enough to take on the responsibility of cooking breakfast. Through some logic of her own, Mom decided that planning and preparing breakfasts for a week at a stretch would be good training. But making breakfasts on top of carrying milk would slow mornings down too much, particularly when we kids had to get to school by 8 o'clock. The trade-off was that she took over most of my barn chores when I made breakfast. This was the latest step in Mom's plan to secure our futures as competent housewives.

As long as I can remember, Mom had been doling out chores around the house. She was determined that my sisters and I would grow up with better preparation to be homemakers than she'd had. Each Saturday she posted lists on the refrigerator.

Here is a list of chores Mom set out for us each weekend:

- Dust the living room furniture
- Shake the rugs
- Dust the floor
- Take fruit jars to the basement
- Sweep down the cellar steps
- Take garbage to the dump
- Clean your room
- Change the sheets on your bed
- Throw dirty clothes down the chute
- Clean the bathroom
- Iron the handkerchiefs
- Practice accordion – 15 minutes

The list was divided into three columns and a column was assigned to each of us girls. Mom must have spent some time thinking about this list each week because the chores assigned changed from week to week, but each list of chores took almost exactly the same amount of time to complete. I was sure of that because I timed it.

Practicing the accordion was the only thing Mom

set a time on. She added it to the Saturday chore list even though we had to practice every day. When we had started taking accordion lessons a couple of years before, we'd all been enthusiastic. Mom thought we'd learn classical music. We kids thought we'd be as good as Myron Floren who played accordion on the Lawrence Welk Show we watched on TV every Saturday night.

After two years, we hadn't progressed much beyond "*Lady of Spain*" and "*Beer Barrel Polka*." Still, we persisted. Fifteen minutes of practice was not enough time to become proficient, but it was as long as Mom could get us to sit down, pick up the fancy accordions that had seemed so glamorous in the beginning, and practice. And when Mom got her mind set on something, we all knew we might just as well do it.

Some chores were so easy they almost didn't count. Taking the fruit jars to the basement, for instance. That took about two minutes. Fruit jars came up from the fruit cellar one or two at a time as Mom planned the upcoming meal and sent us down to retrieve whatever she needed at the moment: a two-quart jar of tomato juice to make tomato soup, a pint of green beans or carrots, a pint of blackberries to serve over ice cream. No doubt Mom was carrying empty jars back to the basement every time she went down herself, but considering Mom drew three to five jars a day from the shelves of the grocery store that was our fruit cellar, there were always jars to carry back to the basement. On Saturday, any jars still on the counter were on the chore list.

Lined up neatly on the shelves, mouths down so spiders and bugs couldn't crawl inside, the empty Mason jars marked the progress of the year until the next canning season. In an ongoing test of how many jars I could carry at once, I tucked jar after jar between my arm and my chest and then looped each finger into the rims of other jars. Up to eight jars in one arm and five in the other made it safely to the basement. I never lost a one.

On an average Saturday, house chores didn't take more than about half an hour. It was only during spring or fall cleaning that we would be at it for a whole day. Then we washed windows and moved furniture to vacuum. Nonetheless, I always liked barn chores better.

Dad never wrote the barn chores down. He just issued our marching orders as we finished breakfast. "Clean out the calf pens," or "Sweep down the cobwebs in the barn," or "Go chop the thistles at the end of the lane." Those chores could take hours, but being outside or around the animals was my preference. Still, I rose to the challenge of housework, just as I rose to the challenge of most assignments, because they were set before me.

This is not to say I always stepped up to these chores like Miss Mary Sunshine. Oh, no. But generally, my resistance to chores took the form of rolled eyes, heavy sighs and grand Do I have to's? Directed to Mom. Never Dad. Except one Saturday. The Saturday Dad tagged me to watch the gate between the barnyard and the field while he hauled manure. Watching gate was one boring job.

After Dad filled the manure spreader, I opened the gate so he could drive through. Once he was outside the barnyard, I closed and latched the gate. While he drove through, I watched to ensure none of the cows snuck out with him. Then I waited for Dad to return, at which point I opened the gate again, he drove through, and I closed the gate. Again. And again. And again.

It was true that my presence kept Dad from having to climb on and off the tractor countless times in the course of the afternoon. And it did ensure the cows didn't get loose.

So the chore was worthwhile. But it was boring. In fact, if you looked in a dictionary, I am fairly certain you would find 'tending the gate' as part of the definition of 'boring.' Depending upon which field Dad was spreading the manure on, the one minute of action required of me might be sandwiched between 15 or 20 or even more minutes of mindless inactivity.

That Saturday afternoon, I convinced myself that while Dad was out spreading a load of manure there was plenty of time for me to run to the house, watch some of the latest *Lone Ranger* episode, and get back to the gate before he returned. As soon as I latched the gate behind him, I raced to the house, flopping on the floor in front of the TV just as the announcer said, "with a cloud of dust and a hearty, hi ho Silver!" That was the last thought I had of the gate until I heard Dad's heavy boots clomping across the kitchen linoleum. I never left the gate again.

My diligence passed on to all other chores.

Unlike tending gate, making breakfast was not boring at all. I poked a finger at the package of sausage in the sink, disturbing the beads of perspiration coating the wrapper. It was completely thawed, so I unwrapped the meat, searched the spice shelf in the cupboard for sausage seasoning and sprinkled a generous coating over the flattened ground meat. The meat squished through my fingers as I kneaded in the spice and formed the neat little patties I stacked on a plate by the stove.

For the fifty-sixth time, I reviewed the menu in my mind, which order to do things, what didn't hurt to sit and what had to be done at the last minute, how to time it. I wanted it to be perfect, just like Mom did it; just like I could do it when Mom helped me.

Whenever I was learning to cook something, Mom was always right there, pulling a spice off the shelf just as I needed it, whisking away the egg shells as soon as I'd cracked them into the bowl, washing bowls and spoons as soon as I was finished with them, wiping up spills as they happened. With her ready assistance and encouragement, there was no cooking project too complicated because there was no way I could fail. At the same time, without Mom there as my ever reliable safety net, I never became exactly confident I could do it well myself, a dilemma I only came to realize many years after I'd been cooking on my own.

With the sausages ready, I turned my attention to the pancakes. Pancakes were no doubt the thing I was best at, next to tomato soup with homemade egg dumplings. Under Mom's watchful eye and helpful hands, I'd made pancakes many times. The recipe was etched in my brain but I still pulled out the stained recipe card just to be sure.

Pancakes
Two cups of flour
Two teaspoons of salt
Two teaspoons of baking powder
Two tablespoons of oil
Two cups of milk
Two eggs separated

I beat the egg whites stiff in their own bowl and then mixed the rest of the batter in another bowl. These could sit until I saw everyone coming up the hill from the barn.

With the bottle of maple syrup warming in a pan of water on the stove, I set the table, poured the tomato juice, and made a pot of coffee. At the last minute, I remembered the butter dish and salt and pepper.

I cannot think how many times we'd all just sat down to eat and Dad would say, "Where's the salt and pepper?" In less than a heartbeat, Mom would be out of her chair to grab the shakers from the cupboard.

Glancing at the clock, I anticipated I had about 10 minutes before I'd see everyone coming up the hill so I turned on the burner to fry the sausages. Just as the sausages achieved the perfect crispy outside, Mom and Dad and my sisters walked in the door, right on schedule. I turned down the heat, put a lid on the frying pan to keep the sausages warm, folded the egg whites into the batter and headed for the basement, pausing as Mom came into the kitchen.

"How are you doing?" she asked as she lifted the lid on the sausage pan.

"Got it under control," I said, watching for her nod of approval before I turned toward the stairs and the big, black griddle.

Fixing meals all on my own seemed a daunting task. Until I had to do it myself, I never entertained the first thought about how Mom did it. How she managed to time everything to arrive at the table hot and perfect at exactly the moment we were ready to sit down was a mystery I started to unravel when I was 10 years old.

A Dangerous Game

"Do you see her?" Sue looked up at me as I clung to the top slat of the gate, craning my neck to see as far as possible.

"No. Maybe she's in the barnyard yet," I suggested, scanning the field between the house and our country schoolyard, staring hard at each of the cows Dad had just let out of the barnyard. We never used to pay attention to the cows, only to the bull, but these days we also had to keep an eye out for one particular heifer.

"Are you sure you'd know her if you saw her?" Sue challenged.

"Pretty sure," I said. One black-and-white cow out of several dozen black-and-white cows? Only Dad was able to tell each and every one from the others. I wasn't absolutely, totally sure, but I thought I could.

"If she is out there and we just don't see her, do you think we can make it?" Jane asked, her voice wavering. We edged through the gate and out into the field, stopping to look again while we were still behind the windbreak line of trees.

"I don't see her yet and we can't wait any longer," I said. "We'll be late."

"Okay," Jane said, taking a deep breath and grabbing hold of Sue's hand. "Let's go."

With that, we took off running, sped along by pumping adrenaline. It was less than a quarter-mile from the fence by the house to the stile over the schoolyard fence. But that's a long, long way when a cow is after you.

As we raced through the knee-deep grass, our hair and lunch boxes flying, the hems of our dresses caught up around our knees, we kept one eye on the cows and one on the schoolyard. The cows that stopped to eat as soon as they came to the first green shoots looked up with mild interest and then dropped their heads for another mouthful of grass. Spring pasture was far more interesting than three little girls chasing across the field.

Before we reached the stile, we spotted the cow of our concern, a heifer less than two years old, breaking into a trot across the field.

"There she is," I yelped. "She's coming! Hurry!"

The heifer was too far away to be a real danger, but my stomach did a flip and I ran faster. We all did.

Jane pushed Sue up the stile steps ahead of her, then we scrambled over. Safe on the other side, we looked back and saw the heifer slow to a walk. We caught our breaths, leaned into each other in relief and broke out laughing. Escaped death once again!

Farms present a wide range of life-threatening circumstances. Our parents warned us about some of these dangers on a regular basis. "Don't go on the highway," Mom said anytime we played in the field north of the house. Mom said *Don't go on the highway* so often that my skin prickled as though shocked by an invisible electric fence anytime I was within 30 yards of that road.

The highway was a real and present danger. We knew this for certain because a little girl who lived across the highway from us, the only child in the neighborhood who was just my age, was struck and killed by a car on this highway, right in front of our lane, when she was only four. Mom would never, never, never let us forget.

Because nothing serious occurred as a result of other fairly obvious dangers, we were cautious but not overly concerned. Take the bull, for instance. A massive, 2,200-pound Holstein, with hulking body and a neck as thick as a 55-gallon drum, the bull spent his days in a stall in the barn. A fine coating of barn dust blanketed the bull's hide, making him look old even though he was in his prime. None of us brushed the dust off or gave him a friendly pat when we passed by his stall like we did with the calves in adjoining pens or the cows when they were in for milking. The same invisible electric warning fence sounded by our parents about the highway kept us on alert around the bull.

The bull escaped from his stall one day when we were playing in the haymow with our cousins. From the safety of the haymow, we peered down the hay chute with a combination of horror and delighted hysteria as the bull worked his way up and down the alleys, cleaning up remnants of hay and grain. In the bizzaro minds of children, this was the kind of happening that just proved how great it was to live on a farm instead of in town like our cousins.

The bull chose to lie down at the base of the ladder, our only means of escape. The lowest doors out of the haymow were a good 20 feet above the ground, an intimidating height none of us was willing to jump. It should be noted that as long as we remained in the haymow, we were perfectly safe, but of course as soon as we could not leave, it was the only thing we wanted to do.

Shouting like lunatics from the haymow doors, we created enough commotion to attract the attention of our parents in the house. Roused from their Sunday afternoon naps, Dad and Uncle Ed came to the barn to rescue us. As a result of that day, I never entered the barn again without bracing my knee against the barn door before opening a one-inch crack and peeking in to see if the bull was loose.

Other circumstances never struck us as dangers at all. We scampered across the roof of the hog shed in games of tag, balanced our way along the two-by-four boards that divided the grain bins in the upper levels of the corn crib, climbed to the top of the silos, 50 feet in the air, where we used pitchforks to clear silage away from the blower when Dad chopped corn and hay to fill the silos. Every building, every field on the farm was open to us for play and work.

But farms do present the possibility of danger whether we recognized it or not. The cows were in this group.

On a dairy farm, heifer calves are raised to join the milking herd. The cow that eventually caused us such trouble started out as one of those darling little calves. All legs and great big, liquid black eyes. Like all the other calves, she sucked hard on our fingers as we dipped her nose in a bucket of warm milk to teach her to drink. Since our chores didn't take long, my sisters and I also played with the calves.

Every year, we watched the boys and girls in the boys' 4-H clubs show their animals at the Fair. Our pleas to show calves fell on deaf ears. Dad was as adamant in his position about boys' 4-H as he was about letting me have a horse. No. No. No. No. No. No matter how often we asked.

So pretending our calves would eventually be show calves became one of our games.

We braided ropes out of binder twine, hooking the knotted twine over nails in the barn walls across from the calf pens and competing to see who could make the smoothest ropes. We fashioned these ropes into halters. When the calves were little, we cornered them in the pens, slipped the halters over their heads, and led them out of the barn. We guided them round the yard as though we were showing them at the county fair.

From time to time, we pretended we were cowboys, practicing our lasso techniques in the pens. Romping around the pens, butting up against us, the calves appeared to have a good time, too.

These games lasted only a short while. The farm offered an endless range of diversions, from chores assigned by Mom or Dad to activities we dreamed up—things like converting the outhouse to a playhouse or staging grand dramas when our cousins came to visit and charging our parents two cents to see our productions. Plus the calves grew up quickly. From about 80 pounds at birth, within a few months, a calf weighed several hundred pounds. A mature Holstein cow weighs 1,300–1,500 pounds.

While most calves outgrew playing just as we kids did, the problem was that even as this particular calf grew to full size, she still loved to play. She scrambled to greet us when we came in the barn, tossing her head and forcing the other calves out of the way so we could scratch her forehead or hug her neck. In just one year, she had reached nearly full size, and while we weighed about 75 pounds and were ready to stop playing, she weighed close to 1,000 pounds and was not.

That's when the real games—and the real potential for danger—began.

One Sunday when the platter was cleared of the last piece of fried chicken, Mom looked around the table and suggested, "Why don't you kids go outside and play."

On any other day, we girls had to do dishes, but on Sundays when we had company and there were other kids to entertain, Mom let us off the hook. This Sunday Aunt Joyce and Uncle Ed and our cousins came to visit, arriving right after we got home from church and just in time to get dinner on the table. When Mom let us loose, we slid off our chairs like our bottoms were greased and charged out the door before she could change her mind.

Once out of the house, we asked our cousins—three boys who matched the three of us girls in ages—"What do you want to do?" We let them choose because they lived in town, which was boring to us, and because they were guests, so it was polite. Donny said, "Let's go down by the creek." That was as good an idea as any, so we raced off down the lane to the Back 40.

When we got to the pasture, the cows were scattered across the east end of the field, grazing or lying in the shade of trees along the creek, chewing their cuds. Their coats glistened clean in the afternoon sun, like a picture in Dad's *Hoard's Dairyman* magazine. We headed to the other end of the pasture, upstream of the cow herd. The cows took no particular notice of us, and we were under standing orders from Dad not to bother them. *Don't make the cows run* were always the last words Dad uttered anytime he knew we were going to be around the herd.

On that summer day, it truly never occurred to any of us anything would happen. If we thought about it at all, we figured there was safety in our numbers. We were wrong.

In the cool shade of trees along the creek, oblivious to the cows, we built sailboats out of bark, sticks and leaves, skimmed stones along the water, and decided to build a dam from bank to bank. We thought we might attract beavers, though we'd never seen one in our creek. None of us paid any attention to the cows and it was only when one left the herd and ambled directly toward us that we took notice.

I didn't recognize the heifer at first. Coming straight at us, we couldn't see the pattern of the black-and-white markings we would all come to know as well as our own faces. When it sank in that this was *the* heifer, I scrambled to my feet. "She's coming," I exclaimed.

"Who's coming?" Donny asked, glancing up as he grabbed another stone and added it to the pile we were amassing in the creek.

"That heifer." The tone of my voice brought my sisters to their feet.

Without hesitating, Jane said, "We have to get out of here. Come on!" The urgency in her voice yanked the boys to attention.

When all six of us stood up at once, the Holstein heifer pulled up short. She studied us. Warily, we watched her.

"What's the big deal?" Johnny asked. The oldest among us, six months older than Jane, Johnny was almost 13 and the closest thing to an older brother I had. Skinny, approaching gangly, he stood with feet apart, hands on hips, like a man but not yet a man. Johnny was ready to back the cow down. Donny and Herm stepped up beside him.

"It's *that* heifer," I repeated with edgy stress, as

though that explained everything, which of course it didn't. "The one that got Mom down."

The boys jerked around to look at me in disbelief. "That's the one that broke Aunt Belle's wrist?" Johnny was incredulous. I nodded, feeling the weight of the realization beating down on all of us like the early summer sun. We all knew this story.

Mom was in the barnyard getting the cows in to milk. She saw the heifer coming toward her and figured she'd stop it by throwing her arm around its neck. The young cow tossed her head and threw Mom off balance, knocking her to the ground. The heifer planted her forehead square in the middle of Mom's chest and pushed her across the manure-covered barnyard. Mom screamed. And screamed. And screamed. Dad raced out from the barn and with one shout of "HEY!" the heifer looked up, looked back at Mom, and trotted off.

When Dad helped Mom to her feet, Mom knocked off the chunks of manure and defended the heifer, "She just wanted to play." Though her wrist hurt, she didn't go to the doctor until a month later when her wrist still hurt. When she learned her wrist was broken, she opted for a brace instead of a cast. That wrist never did heal right.

Coming to the farm for Sunday dinner or for a week's vacation in the summer, our cousins didn't know much about the cows nor were they certain what to do when one came toward them. Still, we'd all been stuck in the haymow when the bull got loose in the barn. He scared the bejeesus out of us. Bulls could be mean; we knew that. But cows weren't a threat. Generally.

As one, we all looked back to the approaching heifer who regarded us with the same steady gaze. She did not seem angry. Just curious. Like she wanted to play. But she wasn't a calf anymore; now she weighed a thousand pounds. We'd had more than one encounter with her, but those times it was always just us girls. Now there were six of us kids. In spite of Jane's alarm, we stood our ground.

It was a standoff worthy of Marshall Dillon in *Gunsmoke*. Stay or run? The heifer took another two steps toward us and began to look in our imaginations every bit as menacing as a bull ready to charge.

I looked at Jane. "What do you think?"

"I don't know." She never took her eyes off the heifer. "Maybe she won't come any closer."

Just as I looked back at the heifer, she took a step, then two. If this was a game of chicken, we lost. "Let's go," Jane said. The six of us turned and ran.

A quick glance backward revealed that as we ran, the heifer began to lope toward us, picking up speed with each step.

"Run for the fence," Jane yelled. We all raced toward the barbed wire fence between the pasture and the corn field. Leaping over ditches, scrambling up banks, Johnny, Donny and I were soon yards ahead.

When we looked back, we saw that Sue and Herm were falling behind and Jane was holding back to stay with them.

"Hurry up! She's gaining on you," Johnny shouted. The heifer was coming at them, moving with purpose in a gait that was not full-out running, but that ate up yards in a hurry.

"They're not going to make it," I panted as I bent over, my hands on my knees, sucking in air.

"Maybe we can get up a tree," Johnny suggested. We scanned the terrain.

"There's one," Donny pointed toward a tree with

fairly low limbs and two trunks forming a crotch we could use as a step up. We ran toward it, screaming at the others to follow.

"Hurry, hurry," we sputtered. Pulling, pushing, jumping, we scampered up the tree like panicked chipmunks. In seconds all six of us were clinging to branches, pulling our feet up just out of reach of the heifer that arrived only moments after the last one of us heaved up to a safe branch. Panting, we caught our breath and lapsed into nervous giggles as the heifer stood looking up at us, bawling.

"We made it," Johnny crowed, kicking at the heifer that stood craning her neck up toward our dangling feet.

We wiggled around on the branches, grappling to find solid seats and secure limbs to hold for balance.

"What's the matter with her?" Herm asked.

"She wants to play," Jane said. None too fond of heights, Jane had one arm wrapped around the trunk while she kept a grip on Sue's arm with her free hand.

"Play?" Donny exclaimed. "More like kill us."

"No, she wants to play. Don't you remember last summer when you came for a week? We braided halters and led the calves around the yard. We used to do that with this heifer when she was little," Jane explained.

"No way!" he said in amazement. The little calves we lassoed when we played cowboy with our cousins bore no meaningful connection to these adult cows.

"Yes, it is. I guess she liked to play. She still thinks she can."

We all looked down at the heifer butting her head against the tree trunk and straining her neck up toward our feet dangling from the branches like fruit ready to pick.

"What are we gonna do?" Herm asked.

We looked around. The barbed wire fence that

marked the safety of the next field was a good 50 yards away. Between our tree and the fence were gullies and a brambly blackberry patch. It may as well have been a mile. We couldn't run there faster than the cow.

"Maybe if we all got down at once, it would scare her away," Donny suggested.

"I don't think so. She came after all of us by the creek," I reminded him. "And all three of us were in the barnyard getting the heifers in when she chased Sue up on the fence."

The boys turned to Sue. "What happened to you?" Herm asked.

Sue didn't answer right away and I jumped in. "It was really funny," I said.

"It was not," Sue glared at me, her lower lip curled in a pout. "It was scary."

"Yeah, but it's funny now," I persisted.

"Come on. What happened?" Herm prodded.

"Okay. The cows were in the lane ready to come in for milking," I began, since it didn't look as though Sue was going to talk.

"It's my story," Sue interrupted.

"Okay, then. Tell it."

"Just let me," Sue glowered, suddenly important in the limelight of our cousins' attention. "The heifers were in the barnyard. Dad said to go chase them into the barn. Then we could open the gate for the cows."

"Usually they just go right in as soon as we open the barn door," I interrupted, hurrying the story along. Sue stared daggers at me and I shut up.

"Most of the calves headed for the barn right away, just like they always do," Sue continued. "But this calf started coming at me. I didn't know what to do, so I just ran."

Donny straddled the branch as he turned to me, "Why didn't you stop her?"

"I didn't even see it happen until Sue was already on the fence and the heifer was butting her. Sue held onto the fence rail. When the heifer butted at her behind, Sue flew up in the air and came back down, still hanging onto the fence. The heifer butted her into the air again and again. Sue held on, screaming her lungs out." I paused, rather enjoying the drama and forgetting for the moment how scared I had been at the time.

"What happened then?" Herm asked, his brown eyes wide open.

"Dad came tearing out into the barnyard with a pitchfork in his hands and a look on his face like I hope to never see turned on me. Dad yelled '*HEY!*' and smacked that heifer across the rump with the pitchfork. She backed right away from Sue and ran."

The boys looked down at the heifer that had taken to eating grass just below our tree. The boys were gaining newfound respect for her size, which looked huge even as we peered down at her from our secure and lofty perches. We drew our feet further up on the limbs.

Turning back to Sue, Johnny asked, "Why didn't you just let go? I bet you'd have flown right over the fence and she couldn't have got you."

Sue's eyes brimmed with tears. "I didn't think to let go. She was going to kill me."

"No, she wouldn't," I interjected, seeing at once the logic of Johnny's suggestion. "You could have just gone over the fence. Besides, Dad was there."

Sue stuck her tongue out at me and we lapsed into silence staring down at the heifer who had just lain down. Right under the tree. She was chewing her cud like she didn't have a care in the world and also like she wasn't going to move. Ever.

"And now we're stuck in this tree," Johnny pointed out the obvious. "What are we going to do?"

We talked about sneaking out of the tree and making a run for it. We looked again at how far away the fence was. We knew we could not all make it. We considered whether we could holler loud enough to get Butch to come; the cows respected the dog. We thought about whether Johnny or Donny could outrun the cow and go get Dad. We sat in the tree for a long time.

Over time, we tore leaves and twigs off the tree and threw them down, pelting the heifer. She looked up, but she just continued to chew her cud, waiting for us to come down and play.

"We can't stay up here forever," Jane observed. Still, we were not coming up with an alternative.

While we were talking, Johnny had been working to tear a limb from the tree. Finally, it broke off and he began poking at the cow. He could barely reach her, so his initial pokes had about as much effect as a fly landing on the heifer's back.

"Hold on to my legs. I'm going to reach down and give her a good poke. Maybe she'll move," he said as he slung his legs over a branch and lowered himself down until he was hanging by his knees. Donny held his brother's legs and I grabbed hold of Johnny's pants pocket.

Johnny poked the cow hard. She looked up. He slapped her twice across the back, as hard as he could.

"She's getting up," Sue squeaked. "Be careful!"

Indeed the heifer was getting up. Standing, she was altogether too close to Johnny who was still hanging by his knees as we scrambled to pull him back up to the limb. But standing, the heifer was tall enough so Johnny could reach her with his stick and slap her. The rest of us took to screeching like a pack of demented squirrels and between the screeches and slaps, the heifer, looking bewildered and dismayed, moved a couple of steps away.

"Keep yelling," Jane yelled. We did. "Keep hitting at her." Johnny hit at the heifer really hard. The heifer started to lope away from the tree, toward the herd.

"Don't make her *run*," I panicked, remembering at the last moment Dad's warnings. No one stopped yelling. The heifer ran.

We had not discussed what we'd do if the heifer moved, but we did not wait a second when we saw she was headed away from us. Johnny and Donny jumped down. Jane swung Sue down by one arm. As fast as we'd gone up the tree we all came down. Then we ran. And we never stopped yelling.

Moments later we dove under the bottom row of barbed wire, rolling to safety on the other side. Once in the cornfield, nerves trickled out in a stream of giggles as we recounted the race to escape the heifer. In bare seconds, the danger wasn't danger at all.

"Come on," Johnny said, "Let's go tell Uncle Harvey." He raced off toward the house with the rest of us keeping up as best we could. On the safe side of the fence, the entire experience became a great adventure.

In time, this heifer joined the milking herd as Number Six. No 'Bessie' or 'Crissie' on our farm. The cows were a business. And Number Six taught us some valuable life lessons.

Lessons like: "Assess the risk and then take action." You can't stay up a tree all day. Or maybe you can.

Or: "Consider the consequences of your actions." If you make friends with an 80–pound calf, it's helpful to have the wherewithal to deal with the 1,200–pound cow.

At the very least, a practical, self-defense lesson like: "Run fast or carry a big stick." From that day on, we kids made sure Butch was with us when we went to the pasture.

Since the whole farm was our playground, it would never have occurred to us to stay out of a field because Number Six was in it. While we may have asked ourselves why Dad didn't get rid of Number Six, we never brought it up to him. After all, we knew where our milk check—and our most exciting games—came from.

The County Fair & the Teddy Bear

Jackson County Fair—July 23–27—The sign hung on the fence at the southeast corner of the fairgrounds. It wasn't a big sign but when it had gone up at the beginning of the summer just as it did every year, I saw it at once. And now, every time we came into Maquoketa to get groceries or books from the library, I read the sign and when I did, butterflies flittered around in my stomach.

I sat up tall and craned my neck as we passed the fairgrounds, searching for any sign of trucks bringing in the midway rides. Nothing. Thoughts of the Fair and my secret plan were so exciting I could barely sit still. Crouching on my knees, I was dangerously close to sticking my head out the window, a real no-no.

"Sit down and keep your head inside," Mom ordered for the thousandth time. "There won't be anybody there for another two weeks."

Sometimes it was as though she could read my mind, I thought as I flopped down on the seat and dangled my arm out the window, letting my hand float on the wind current. I fiddled with the window vent until it directed the hot July air straight on my face. My hair flipped on the breeze and strands flew into my eyes and mouth.

"What days are we going to the fair, Mom?" I asked, just the same as I asked every time we came to town. Ready to put my plan into action, I knew the fair could not come soon enough. "Can we come every day?"

"Oh, honey, we won't be here every day but we'll come in a few times." Mom breathed an exasperated sigh. We had asked and she had told us this, as well, just under a thousand times.

"I'm going to win the pony this year," Sue shouted from the back seat.

"No, I am," I countered, without even looking back.

"Are not. I am!"

"Uh-uh."

Sue and I batted retorts at each other like a game of badminton. Playing along disguised the fact that this year I didn't care nearly so much about the pony. I had a bigger plan for winning, one I could control.

Winning the Shetland pony given away at the fair every year had been my fondest desire. We could enter as many times as we wanted, and Sue and Jane and I filled out slip after slip, folding each one in a tangle of origami-like folds before depositing it in the barrel by the grandstand, as though the elaborate folds would attract the hand of the person who did the drawing.

In all the years I dreamed of having a pony of my own, it never once occurred to me to tell Dad I'd buy one with my own money. Dad farmed with horses when he first came on the farm. I vaguely remembered those horses though they were gone by the time I was four years old and it's possible I remember the horses only because Mom took pictures. From time to time, I begged openly for a horse and Dad—who bought a tractor as soon as he could afford one—never hesitated to share his position on horses.

"Squirt," he'd say, "A horse is good for nothing. When you have a horse, here's what happens. At the beginning of winter, you have a barn full of hay and a horse. When spring rolls around, you have a horse and a pile of shit. No hay."

So my annual quest for a horse began and ended with the possibility of winning a pony at the fair. I realized that with the pony, my fate was entirely in someone else's hands. To win, to be sure I would win, I needed to employ my own skill.

This year I had my eye on winning something else—a teddy bear on the midway. I crossed my legs Indian-style, threading my fingers in and out between my toes, in a vain effort to sit still. Barely able to contain my excitement, I turned toward the window so Mom wouldn't read the secret on my face. No one knew about this secret. No one.

"I am too going to win," Sue blurted again, hanging over the back of the seat and punching me in the arm.

"Cut it out!" I slapped at Sue's hand.

"That's *enough*." Mom ended our squabble. "I'll drop you off at the library while I get groceries. Pick out some books and I'll be back in a half-hour."

"Okay, Mom. We'll be waiting," I called over my shoulder as Sue and I jumped out of the car and ran up the steps to the library. We skidded to a stop as soon as we got to the heavy doors opening to the library's cool marble floors and huge oak checkout desk. Our chatter turned off like a spigot when we moved reverently between the stacks of books. The dry, dusty book smell surrounded me like a welcoming blanket.

I wandered through the bookshelves, trailing my fingers along the leather spines, and finally sat cross-legged on the floor next to the Zane Grey section. I pulled *Riders of the Purple Sage* off the shelf, opened it on my lap and idly turned the pages. The words blurred in front of my eyes; my mind was on the fair. In fact, my mind had been on the fair all summer.

I looked forward to everything about the fair. The grandstand shows where one year Gene Autry picked ME out of the crowd and had ME stand by him on the stage. His horse Champion nibbled on my cheek and everyone laughed. I would never forget that. Sitting with Dad on a stool at one of the concession stands under the grandstand, having a hamburger. The Methodist Church had the best food overall, but the American Legion men grilled the best hamburgers. I could already smell the fried grease and my stomach growled thinking about it. I glanced up to see if the librarian had noticed. She hadn't looked up and I returned to leafing through the western.

At the fair, we wandered through the cattle barns, watching with thinly disguised envy as the kids in FFA and boys' 4-H clubs got their steers and sheep and pigs and horses ready to show. We wanted to show animals, but Dad was against it. No matter what we said, we never convinced him. Jane and Sue and I were members of a girls' 4-H club and our fair entries ran through a cycle of sewing, gardening, cooking and home furnishing projects. We waited impatiently to see if our work earned a blue ribbon or red. I didn't even want to think about getting a third-place white ribbon.

Every year during the fair, we scouted out the commercial vendor exhibits, snatching up all the free stuff—pencils and key chains and yardsticks—until we had a treasure bag of valuable booty. At one end of the vendor building was one of the magical wonders of the fair—a giant faucet that floated in the air, unconnected to any pipe or wire, yet pouring a heavy stream of water into a barrel below. Even after I was old enough to understand how it worked, I stood transfixed at the Culligan exhibit each year, straining to see the plastic tube. I never could.

I leaned back against the stack of books and sighed. It was magic. It was glorious. It was *The Fair*.

Above all else, though, the midway was the big attraction. The midway was loud and bright, dangerous and romantic. Thrill rides: the roller coaster, the Octopus, the Tilt-a-Whirl. Even the Teacup ride taken to extreme could be too much. Sue learned that one year after she rode it time and again and wound up barfing up the hot dog she'd just eaten.

And the Ferris Wheel always stopped at the top at least once during the ride. From there you could see all over town and out into the country. As the seat swung back and forth, my knees turned to water and I clutched the bar that held us in the bucket. I thought soaring so high in the air must be like flying in the airplanes I watched leave white trails in the sky over our farm.

The house of mirrors. The freak show with midgets and tattooed women and Jo-Jo the Dog Faced Boy, and the barker encouraging all the men to come in and see the dancing girls.

The games where, for just one quarter, you could win a giant teddy bear. For just one quarter!

I watched these games every year. I saw teenaged boys win stuffed animals for their girlfriends. I saw kids littler than me win funny hats and goldfish in bowls and Hawaiian leis. This year when the fair came to Maquoketa, I would win my very own teddy bear. I had been planning it for months. The idea planted itself in my head in the spring, and throughout the summer it had been growing and growing until now I could hardly go a day without imagining how I would accomplish this incredible feat.

I'd watched those games enough to know that you really didn't win a teddy bear with just one quarter unless you were really, really, really lucky. Plus I wanted to go on rides and eat cotton candy and caramel apples and hot dogs. So I knew I had to save my money.

And I did. All summer. I saved my allowance and any money I earned picking potato bugs off the potato plants or giving Dad a ride to the barn in the red coaster wagon or from any other scheme we concocted to earn a little extra money. Each week I emptied out my piggybank on my bed, sorted the coins into neat little piles and counted it up. I'd done it again last night and with the fair just a couple of weeks away, I had amassed a fortune. I had $7.75. By the time the fair came to town, I would have Eight Whole Dollars!

I could hardly wait. I did not share my plan with anyone. I had made my decision on my own. I saved my money on my own. And I was going to win a teddy bear. On my own.

"Come on. Let's go." Sue nudged me with her toe. I looked up, surprised to see her standing with a load of books in her arms. "Mom's outside."

Scrambling to my feet, I grabbed a few more Zane Grey books off the shelf and ran to check them out. Maybe reading would make the days until the fair go faster.

No luck. The days crawled by with all the speed of the box turtle I'd found one day by the creek. But eventually, the fair did arrive and sure enough, I found myself walking through the livestock barns and picking up the free stuff in the vendor building and registering for the Shetland pony just because that was what I always did.

And just as I'd planned for many months, I walked up and down the midway and looked at all the games. Each game was run by a "carny," a man with long hair and tattoos who always seemed to look dirty, who was scary yet attractive in an exotic sort of way. More than once I thought about running away with the fair.

I'd been up and down the midway a few times with Jane and Sue, looking at the rides, planning what we'd go on and when. Each time they suggested we try one, I begged off. My mind was set on figuring out the right game to play to win the teddy bear. I kept my money tight in my fist for that alone.

Games with only a few bears hanging on the frame were out. No doubt they were so hard no one ever won. Games with only small bears weren't for me either. My prize would be a big bear. Finally, I found the game. It was kind of like shuffleboard bowling. For a quarter, you got three tries to knock down all the pins. As soon as I could ditch Jane and Sue, I headed back to that stand.

From about 15 feet away, I watched others try the game and win. Or they tried and walked away empty-handed. I wanted to take my chance but I was afraid. Even though there were three lanes to play, I didn't want to play when anyone else was there. It didn't take long for the carny running the game to see me looking. "Come on, kid," he called out. "Give it a try. Lots of people win here!" That was all I needed.

Trying not to appear too eager, I handed the carny a quarter and he gave me the discs. I held one of the discs for a moment to get a feel for the weight and then with some hesitation slid it toward the pins. A couple of pins fell, boosting my confidence greatly. In a rush, I slid the remaining two discs toward the pins. I didn't get all the pins down, but I got many of them.

I grinned up at the carny, confident I could pull it off the next time. "I want to do it again," I said.

"Sure. Here you go," he said, smiling back encouragement as he handed me three more discs.

I got a better feel for the game this time and almost got all the pins down. It was not as easy as I'd thought it would be, but I wasn't discouraged.

"You better try it one more time," the carny urged. "You almost got them down that time."

"Okay," I said, handing over another of my hard-earned quarters in exchange for another chance to win the coveted bear.

I tried again. And again. And again. Each time I came so close, each time the carny encouraged me to just try it one more time. Within minutes, I wasn't thinking of rides or food; I was thinking only about the teddy bear. I just had to win. Quarters led to dollars. As each quarter passed from my hand to the carny, anxiety nibbled at the edges of my stomach and desire forced it back. If I tried just one more time, I knew I'd knock the pins down and the teddy bear would be mine.

Before I realized what had happened, I had handed the carny my entire eight dollars.

"Too bad, kid," the carny said. "I was sure you had it. If you just get another quarter, I bet you'll get it next time."

The carny's words broke through the hypnotic fog I'd wandered in as I handed over quarter after quarter. I couldn't believe it! In less than half an hour, I'd spent every penny I'd worked all summer saving. And I didn't win. I stared at the carny stupefied. How? . . . What? . . . How?

As the carny turned his attention to another rube, and that is exactly what I realized I was, I turned away, shuffling my feet in the trampled midway dust. Defeat weighed heavy on my shoulders and the shouts of carnies yelling to attract passersby to their games echoed hollow and mocking in my ears. Could everyone see what a fool I was?

Blinking back tears, I stumbled down the midway as fear rose in my gut. How could I tell my folks? If I'd won the teddy bear, playing the game with all my money would have been justified. At least I thought so.

It hadn't occurred to me yet what I would do for the rest of the fair. My folks weren't the kind to just give me more money. We could spend what we earned—although I knew they'd think I'd been foolish wasting all my money on the carnival games—Lord knows with each passing step I felt more foolish all on my own—but I was certain they wouldn't give me more money either. It had never really occurred to me that I would miss out on rides and cotton candy and hot dogs. My plan was to win the teddy bear and have money for the rest. Eight dollars was enough money to have it all. I convinced myself I wouldn't have minded no rides and no cotton candy and no other games if I'd had my prize. But now, I had *nothing*.

I didn't want to see anything else at the fair. I didn't care what ribbons I got on my 4-H projects. I was sick and I stumbled back to Mom in shock.

Collapsing into her arms, tears streaming down my face, I spilled out my tale of woe in breathless hiccups. "Mom, ... I tried to win a teddy bear ... and I didn't ... and I spent all my money."

Mom pulled me onto her lap, wrapped her arms

around me and held me tight, as she crooned words of comfort. "Oh, honey. You must really have wanted to win."

Mom didn't say I was foolish. Neither did Dad. They didn't have to. I knew it. Embarrassment at my own stupidity stuck in my throat like a piece of meat eaten too fast, too big and too tough to swallow.

Mom and Dad did fill in for the things I would have missed having spent all my money on the first day, but the fair was ruined for me anyway. I couldn't let it go. I dragged around like a whipped dog, disconsolate, well after the carnies packed up the rides and left for the next town, long after the smell of grilled hamburgers no longer hung on the July air.

Finally, Mom couldn't stand my pathetic moping anymore and she took me to the Woolworth Five & Dime on Main Street. Focused as I was on winning a teddy bear at the fair, I had never paid much attention to the bears lining the store shelves. These bears were more glorious than any I could have won, and Mom bought the one of my choice. Hugging the big brown-and-gold bear to my chest, I snuggled up against Mom all the way home.

At that moment I thought I was happy; I believed I was happy. I wanted a bear, and I had a bear. But being given a bear from the store was not the same as winning it on my own. It was most definitely not the same as earning it. I knew it then and I know it now.

That summer, I was captured by the desire to get something for nothing. Caught in that desire, I failed to see that the midway games—even those that appeared to be based on skill—were really games of chance, contests designed to favor the carnival, matches more likely to be lost than won. Even though I was raised on common sense, knowing that I had to earn whatever I received, I followed the siren song of that desire. My pursuit of that teddy bear demonstrated in a way I could not miss how gullible I could be, how easily I could lose sight of common sense, how quickly I could be seen as foolish to my parents, to myself. These were lessons hard to learn and impossible to forget.

After many years, I still see the fair as a highlight of the summer, but I keep my money in my pocket when I pass the carnies and hear their beguiling calls. I remember the Jackson County Fair and the illusive teddy bear.

Options

The long shelf of Nancy Drew mysteries constituted more than half of our home library. While sitting cross-legged on the floor in front of the bookshelf, I had considered all the titles. So many options. Which one to choose? Since I had read some volumes at least three times, the question was really whether to pick one I couldn't remember at all or a more familiar one. I forgot most story details within weeks of reading them and as a result could return again and again, reading our books with alternating feelings of stomach-clenching suspense and not-to-worry familiarity. Today I chose a comfortable world. *"The Whispering Statue"* was a favorite.

When I pulled the volume off the shelf that morning, I'd been intent on finding a quiet place to curl up, but I opened the book and began reading at once. I'd moved barely five feet when I was drawn so deeply into the action on the pages that I stopped moving and stood lost in another world, a world of mysteries and clues and discovery where Nancy Drew grabbed me by the hand to race along in her life of adventure.

Now I stood, leaning against the wall, book in one hand, my other arm crooked behind my back, my fingers clutching the door frame. It is another fluke of my brain that when I read, I am aware of little else around me. So I didn't hear Jane and Sue until they were tearing up the stairs in front of me.

"It's mine!" Jane yelled over her shoulder as she hit the stairs, bounding up two at a time.

"It's not either. It's mine. Give it to me or I'll tell Mom." Sue skidded around the corner from the living room, snapping at Jane's heels. Sue had almost no chance of getting whatever it was they were fighting over, but she was as persistent as the bull thistles that defied our hoes when Dad sent us down the lane to chop the prickly giants growing wild in the pasture.

"You'll never get it," Jane gasped as she made it to the top of stairs, tore past me into the upstairs bedroom and turned, slamming the door.

"Will too. You just wait," Sue screeched. She dove toward Jane just as Jane threw all her weight against the door and it crashed closed. On my fingers.

The sound of my fingers crunching was drowned out as Sue hammered on the door, throwing threats at the top of her lungs.

The sound of my screams was covered by Jane's near-hysterical laughing as she leaned against the door, shoving back against Sue's equal and opposite force.

Sue shoved; the door opened a quarter-inch; my fingers pulsed and I pulled.

Jane shoved back; the door firmly closed; my fingers ground into the space by a hinge.

Every nerve in my body fired like a lightening strike, and I shrieked. "My hand. My hand. *My hand!*" I knew there was no blood in my face any more, certain as I was it was all draining out my fingers.

My screams penetrated Sue's ears at last. She looked at me and went pale. "Stop pushing, Jane," she bellowed. "Carol's hand is in the door."

There is a unique difference in the sound of children's screams that allows mothers to differentiate between play and danger. Mom heard excruciating pain in my voice, and she materialized at the top of the stairs as if by magic.

Half carrying, half dragging me to the kitchen sink, Mom turned the water faucet on full blast and thrust my throbbing hand under the ice cold stream. "Hold it here," she shouted. Or she may have whispered. I don't know which; her voice came to me as though she were a long, long way off.

"I can't," I sobbed. "It *hurts*." My knees were rubber. My stomach watery. Swallowing hard to keep back the bile that rose in waves in my throat, I rested my head on the cool edge of the sink, letting the tears cascade down my cheeks and drip on the floor.

With one arm wrapped under my armpits, her leg wedged like a seat under my behind, Mom held my hand under the water. "You're going to be okay," she repeated. "This water will make it feel better." After a minute she asked, "Can you wiggle your fingers?"

I had yet to even be able to *look* at my hand; I didn't even know if I still *had* my fingers. Her question made me realize my fingers must still be on my hand. "It hurts," I whimpered.

"I know it does. But come on. Let me see you wiggle your fingers."

Moving my fingers didn't seem possible, let alone wise. What if I couldn't move them? What if moving them made it hurt more? Maybe it was better not to know. I clasped the wrist of my mangled hand in the rigid grip of my good hand, afraid that if I let go, blood would spurt out or my hand would fall off.

"Come on. Move them. Let's just see," Mom urged.

Lifting my head, I forced myself to look at my hand. I expected to see mangled meat. The damaged fingers curled toward my palm and bore sharp, white ridge grooves where they'd been pinched in the door. Remarkably, beyond a few drops seeping out around the fingernails, blood was not flowing down the drain in buckets. Cautiously, I flexed one finger and then another. It was a miracle. They all moved. I gulped and looked up at Mom. "I can move them," I whispered.

"That's good." Mom straightened up, visibly relieved. "Now straighten them way out and let's look." From Mom's practical perspective, once we'd established long-term viability, the emergency was over. According to Mom, pretty much any ailment could be solved with cold water, vinegar or Epsom salts.

That was her solution the day I came limping into the house, sobbing, having just jumped off a fence where I landed barefoot on a nail sticking out of a discarded piece of lumber. My sisters and cousins jumped around like flighty grasshoppers, excited by the blood and my tears. Blood from the deep puncture wound trailed behind me across the green linoleum kitchen floor. Mom grabbed me under the arms, swooping me up onto the kitchen counter next to the sink. The toes of my foot had curled in toward the sole of my foot in a reflex reaction against the pain, and I watched as my blood oozed clean red out of the hole and streamed down the drain in a flood of cold water.

Mom washed away layers of dirt, inspected the hole and declared, "We need to soak it in Epsom salts. Keep your foot under the water while I get a bucket ready."

As Mom submerged my foot in the hot water, she kept up a distracting stream of commentary. "Grandma Denter taught me about Epsom salts. It really works. Here, let me get you a cookie and a glass of milk. Did you know vinegar will cure a sore throat, poison ivy and sunburn?" I stared at her in disbelief. "Well, it will."

For the rest of the morning, I remained in the kitchen, soothed by Mom's ministrations of Epsom salts and cookies. And it did work, that time and many times more throughout my childhood, though how I avoided tetanus all those years, I'll never know. In the world of day-to-day ailments, Mom operated, quite successfully as a matter of fact, as though there wasn't much a doctor could do that she couldn't take care of just as well with Epsom salts, cold water or vinegar.

I couldn't see that Epsom salts or vinegar would do anything for my fingers, though. The cold water was helping some, but blood thumped like a timpani in my ears and in my fingers as I inched the tips straight out. Blood pooled and caked black around the edges of my middle fingernail. The nails of both my middle and ring fingers were already a deep purple, and my index fingernail wasn't looking so good either. My entire hand was bright red, which Mom assured me was from the cold water. She was convinced I would not lose my fingers or my hand. I was not so sure.

While I was getting immediate medical attention from Mom, Jane raced out to the barn to tell Dad, omitting, I'm pretty sure, the part about her slamming the door on my hand. By the time Mom had persuaded me I would live, Dad strode into the house.

Dad's solutions were more personal, and to be honest, unorthodox. On more than one occasion, for instance, he blew cigarette smoke in my ear to cure an ear ache. It worked.

"Better let me take a look at that hand, Squirt," Dad said. He led me outside where he sat down on the bench in the breezeway between the house and garage and pulled me up on his lap. Dad smelled of clean dust from the corn he was grinding for the cows.

As soon as I was on his lap, tears streamed down my face again. My hand hurt like crazy and I flinched as he took hold of my fingers. Considering how rough and calloused Dad's hands were, his warm touch wrapped me in reassuring safety.

"Wiggle your fingers," he said. I didn't tell him Mom already made me do that, because Dad was the ultimate authority. Tentatively, I wiggled each finger.

"That's good. They're not broken," he confirmed. "But you're gonna lose those fingernails."

"It really hurts, Dad," I said, dissolving in a renewed flood of tears that formed dark, wet blotches on his shirt.

"I expect it does," he agreed. "There's blood behind the nails. That's why they're getting all black."

I considered my fingers. My nails would get black. They would fall off. Things just got worse. A wave of self-pity for my poor hand swept over me, and a fresh bucket of tears fell.

"There is something we can do about that," he said when I'd cried myself out.

I looked up at him, my spirits bright with both faith and hope. Dad always knew another way, usually a better way. Once I'd gotten ringworm, a red circle of scabby pimples on my forearm by my elbow. Maybe I caught it from a cow, Dad said. He took me to the doctor in Preston who looked it over carefully and pronounced that the only way to get rid of it was to pull out each and every hair on my arm and then use a special salve every day for two weeks.

My mouth went dry, dropping open in horror at the very idea of pulling out all my hair. A blanket of fine, silky hair had covered my forearms as long as I could remember. I looked up at Dad, telegraphing panic. Dad just looked at doctor. "The hell you say," he snorted. "There's more than one way to skin a cat," he said, and we left.

Dad was none too taken with higher education. He finished eighth grade in a one-room country school and never went to high school. He learned everything else he needed to know working. It was just such ideas as the doctor put forward that confirmed his skepticism. And assured that he didn't send us to a doctor on any regular basis. "Paper don't care what you print on it," he said more than once, summarizing his thoughts on book learning.

When we got outside, Dad said, "That's not the only way. I know at least two other ways to get rid of ringworm, and damn, you don't have to pull out any hair."

"What are they?" I asked, grateful forever that Dad didn't leave me with the doctor.

"One way," he said, "is to smear cow shit on the spot every day. That will kill it." He looked right at me when he said this and never blinked. "The other way is to use the same salve we use on the cows when they get it. You can decide when we get home."

I climbed into the pickup truck, my arm crooked so I could clearly see the crusty red ringworm circle, a circle completely covered with hair. All the way home, I thought about pulling out each individual hair.

Dad shook his head solemnly when he shared the

doctor's comments with Mom, "The doctor said we'd have to pull out all her hair."

Mom said, "Oh, no! Can you imagine?" She shook her head and returned to the bread she was kneading, reinforced in her own doubts about doctors.

I thought about pulling out the hair. I thought about having cow shit smeared on my arm every day. I thought about being treated with cow salve.

"I think we should use what works on the cows," I said at last. Dad nodded and we went to the barn to get the salve. The ringworm cleared up in no time.

Now my hand hurt like a son of a gun. If Dad had a solution for this, I wanted to know it. "It hurts horrible," I whimpered, wallowing in my sorry state. "How do you make it stop?"

Gingerly, Dad held my most damaged middle finger, which even swollen as it was almost disappeared between his huge fingers. "It's the blood pushing against the nail that makes it hurt. The way to make it stop hurting is to take a drill and make a little hole in the nail. That will let the blood come out. The pressure will be off and it will feel better."

"*What?*" I gulped. At the mention of the word 'drill,' I wanted to yank my hand back to safety. I envisioned my finger under the drill bolted to the bench in Dad's workshop. I envisioned the drill, high pitched and shrill, in the dentist's office. My back went stiff and I nearly skidded off his lap in a desperate attempt to escape. My tears dried up like a faucet turned off.

Dad didn't move. He kept his arms around me. He held my damaged fingers in his hands. He sat waiting for me to absorb this horrifying thought.

As I thought about it, maybe my fingers didn't hurt

so bad. Not enough to keep crying. Certainly not enough to have Dad drill through my fingernails.

"I'll think about it," I said, and I leaned my head back against his shoulder for a few minutes. At last I tilted my head up so I could look in his eyes and asked, "Would I still lose my fingernails?"

"Yup. It just wouldn't hurt so much as now."

I thought about it some more and then scooted off his lap. I discovered that if I held my hand up above my shoulder it didn't throb quite so much. So I walked around most of the rest of the day like the Statue of Liberty. I did lose my fingernails. But I was going to anyway. I decided it was nice to know that there were options, nicer still to know what those options were, and the best to be able to decide for myself which one to take.

"I Bet You A Million Bucks"

For all but one year of my eight years in country school, I was the only one in my grade. Most of the time I felt a little smug about it, but sometimes I wondered what it would be like to have someone in my class, someone who had the same assignments, someone who might be a best friend. When I thought about those things, I'd get a little lonesome. But one year there was another kid in my class; his name was Virtus. That year I learned to be more careful with both wishes and words. That year I learned an important lesson about values and how sometimes they can come into conflict.

That morning, just like on the first day of school every year, my sisters and I prepared to head off for school, dressed in the new dresses Mom sewed for us over the summer. We always wore dresses to school except on cold and snowy days when we wore dresses with long pants under them. After we ate breakfast and lined up for the first-day-of-school pictures Mom always took, we grabbed our lunch pails and ran through the alfalfa stubble of the field between our house and the school, dodging grasshoppers and chasing butterflies. We climbed over the stile to the schoolyard, where grass was already dry from the summer heat.

As soon as we were all at our desks, Miss Fowler introduced Irving and Virtus, her hands resting lightly on the shoulders of two boys as tall as she. But that wasn't saying much because Miss Fowler was only a little over five feet herself. Their names, their black hair and dark eyes, everything about them was strange. But most intriguing to me was when Miss Fowler said, "Virtus is in fourth grade." Fourth grade was my grade!

While the familiar words of the Pledge of Allegiance rolled automatically out of my mouth, I eyed the new kids. Their pin-straight hair was cut as though someone had put bowls over their heads and cut right around. I expect this is exactly what their dad did, and I snickered. One of our hired men was going on a date one Friday night and needed a haircut. Dad said he could take care of that. As the hired man sat on a chair in the middle of the kitchen, Dad put a bowl right over that young man's head and cut neatly around the edges. The result was not what the hired man expected. He skipped his date. And he never let Dad come near him with scissors again.

What was most surprising about Virtus and Irving, though, was that they were dirty. Not just dirt under their fingernails, but dirt on their clothes, on their necks, in their ears. In fact, I couldn't stop looking at the black grit built up in Virtus's ears.

Mom was cast from the 'cleanliness is next to Godliness' mold. The day didn't go by that she didn't yell at us as we were getting ready, "Make sure you wash your neck and in your ears. You don't want potatoes to grow in there!" In fact, that must have been the case with all the kids in our neighborhood because everyone arrived at school with clean clothes and scrubbed hands, faces, necks, ears. I didn't know what to think of someone who came to school dirty.

I couldn't think about this for long. We all got right down to the work of the day. Miss Fowler had assignments for each grade—penmanship, math, a new chapter in history. How she kept us all going at the same time, I don't know. Sometimes it must have seemed to her she was like that man we watched on the Ed Sullivan Show, the man who spun plates on the top of sticks, getting one plate spinning, running to get another plate spinning, then racing back to the first one to give it another spin, and on and on. How long could he keep them all going before one or more crashed to the ground? Miss Fowler seldom let anything fall.

While we worked at our desks, Miss Fowler had each class come to the front of the room to do their specific problems on the blackboard, read or recite. Meanwhile all the rest of us worked at our desks under the watchful eyes of President Washington, who gazed at us from his picture at the front of the room, and President Lincoln, who observed us from the north wall. I liked school. There was always something new to learn.

The sun that shone in the east windows and warmed our backs at the beginning of the day moved along to shine over our left shoulders. Before long, it was time for recess and Miss Fowler excused us for a half-hour.

In a country school where you might have only a handful of students in the entire school, the playground is a melting pot. For a game of baseball or Red Rover or Pom Pom Pull Away, you need everybody, no matter what age, no matter what background, no matter what capability. Virtus and Irving were drawn in immediately.

Over the next few days and weeks, I learned that Virtus and his family moved around a lot. He'd been in a lot of schools. He bragged about all the places he had been and things he had done. While there wasn't any real reason not to believe what he was saying, most of the time what he said was just so outlandish I ignored it.

One day we took our lunch pails out under the box elder trees to eat. Dust coated the grass. The late September sun was hot but we didn't pay any attention to that. My grandma used to say, "There's no sense being cold if you don't have a sweater." Same way with the heat.

My lunch pail held pancake sandwiches, a banana, a brownie, and a thermos of milk from our own cows. I loved the pancake sandwiches Mom made by rolling up leftover pancakes from breakfast spread with butter and sprinkled with sugar. Eating these sandwiches was like eating dessert.

Virtus had a peanut butter sandwich. That was it. He never had much to eat and always seemed hungry. I felt bad about that so I shared some of mine.

"Do you want this brownie?" I gestured at the thick brownie wrapped in wax paper.

"Yeah. That would be great!" He snatched it so fast I didn't have time for a second thought.

"How about some milk?"

"Sure." He drained my thermos before I had a chance to get any myself.

I held tight to the banana. I knew I'd have to be careful what I offered him in the future.

With no prospect of more food in sight, Virtus lay back on the grass and began tossing a baseball up in the air with one hand and catching it with the other. "I bet I can throw this ball from here and get it over the top of the school," he said.

"Oh, you cannot," I said, leaning back against the tree trunk to enjoy the banana.

"Can too. I've done it lots of times," Virtus said.

"Oh, you have not." I flicked a box elder bug off my shoulder. "I've seen you throw and there's no way you'd even get the ball as far as the school, let alone clear the roof." Okay, I knew he could get it as far as the school, but who cared?

"I bet I can. Want to bet?" he challenged, sitting up and turning to look right at me.

"Sure I'll bet," I said. "I bet you 10 cents you can't." Ten cents was my whole week's allowance.

"I bet you $100 I can," he countered with an impressive figure.

"I bet you a million dollars you can't," I threw out the most incomprehensible number of all time.

Betting a million bucks was something my sisters and I did all the time. Betting a million bucks was a signal that the bettor was so sure of herself there was no contesting it. Betting a million bucks was the guaranteed way to stop a discussion and make the other person back down. Besides, even on a 50-cent bet or a $1 bet we understood there was no money changing hands. None of us had any money regardless of who won. Bets were just talk.

"Done!" Virtus yelled, a grin lighting up his face, his dark eyes dancing. "I take that bet. I'm gonna win a million bucks!" He jumped to his feet and strutted around me like a little Banty rooster.

A tight little knot began to form in my stomach. Something in the way he said that made me think he didn't realize betting was just for fun. I eyed him. Still, there was no way he could throw the ball that far. I kept up the show.

"Huh uh. You're gonna owe *me* a million bucks," I countered. "You have to throw it from here, and it can't even touch the school at all," I began to put parameters on the bet for protection.

"Just watch me," he said. He paced back and forth between the trees. He looked at the school. He squinted at the sun. He licked his finger and held it in the air. That was a joke since there wasn't any wind at all. He tossed the ball gently in the air a couple more times.

"Are you ready for this?" he asked, grinning at me. Without waiting for my answer, he took one last long look at the school roof, drew his arm back and followed through, releasing the ball in a high sailing arc with a power I'd never seen before. The ball went up; it was high enough. The ball kept going; it was far enough. As the ball flew, the knot in my stomach grew, and as I heard the ball thud to the ground on the other side of the school, the knot was tight as a noose.

For the first time I realized I could be in real trouble. Even though betting was just a game to us, giving your word wasn't. While that might seem like a small breakdown in logic, I'd given my word and I knew that now I owed Virtus a million bucks.

"Ha!" he laughed. "Ha, ha, ha!" he leaped in happiness at a truly great throw. "You owe me a million bucks. You owe me a million bucks! I'm RICH!"

"I do not," I tried, my voice weak. "Nobody ever gets a million bucks." Even as I said it, my mind raced ahead to think about where I might actually get a million dollars. Nobody had that kind of money. I knew it. But not paying on the bet, not coming through on my word was more impossible.

"You do, too. You owe me a million bucks and you have to pay it or I'll *tell*," he threatened as he stood, eyes narrowed, nose just inches from mine.

I couldn't let him tell. Everyone would laugh. Everyone would say I was stupid. Miss Fowler would tell Mom and Dad, and they'd think I was horrible. I could already see the disappointment on their faces. I'd never be able to look them in the eye again.

"Well, I don't have it WITH me," I blustered, stalling to grasp even a minute to think my predicament through. "Tomorrow," I offered with a whole lot more confidence than I felt. Virtus glared suspiciously at me for long seconds before he uttered, "Okay," wheeled and stalked away.

I sat through the rest of my classes that day, my stomach tying itself into tight knots. I felt every bit like the last time I threw up. Meanwhile, Virtus spent the rest of the day sprawled in his desk, smirking at my discomfort.

After school, Jane and Sue raced across the field for home, but I lagged behind, my legs getting heavier with each step. Grasshoppers jumped out from under my feet, landing steps ahead in the alfalfa stubble. Their leaps seemed way too happy in my opinion. I kicked up dust. That night the knots in my stomach got bigger and bigger. I had to get the money, but how?

As I lay in bed, I concluded that I'd have to pay Virtus the money I owed a little at a time. Even then, coming up with a million dollars could take the rest of the year. My allowance was NOT going to cover this.

The only person who had money in our family was Dad. Could I ask him for it? No way. If I'd heard him say once, I'd heard him say a million times, "Don't spend money you don't have." I could never admit I'd been so stupid as to bet away money I didn't have. And such an amount; I would die of shame first. And I could not tell Mom. She didn't have any money that I knew of, and she'd tell Dad.

I would have to break my word or steal the money

from my dad. Which was worse? At the moment, it seemed that breaking my word was worse because two of us—Virtus and I—would know about it. If I stole from my Dad, maybe I'd only have my poor conscience to contend with. Maybe Dad would never know.

Gradually a plan formed in my mind. It was this. Dad wore work clothes on the farm. He had nails and a pocketknife and a handkerchief in the pockets of his work clothes. When he went to town, he changed clothes. He had loose change in the pocket of his dress trousers and those trousers hung on a hook in his bedroom closet. He never took the change out of the pockets. It should be a simple matter to slip into his closet when he and Mom were in the barn milking and take some of that change. Not all of it, of course. My plan would never work if he expected to find change in his pocket and none was there. But a little every day or so. That shouldn't be noticeable. It seemed like a plan that could work.

By the time I climbed over the stile from our field to the schoolyard the next morning I was almost certain the plan would work and I'd begun to resign myself to living life as a thief. Virtus waited for me by the stile.

"Where's my money?" he hissed. "You owe me that money and you have to pay it."

"I don't have it." I squirmed. "I'm working on it. Tomorrow."

Virtus's mouth twisted into a frown. "You have to pay me or I'll *tell*," he threatened again. Telling was the worst. We both knew it.

"I will," I insisted, "but I can't pay all of it at once." I hated him right then but I'd begun to like me even less.

"Okay, but I better see some of it tomorrow." Virtus

growled as he stuck his hands in the pockets of his dirty bib overalls and stomped away.

School meant very little to me at that moment. I could think only of the money I owed. My plan was trickier than it might at first seem because I couldn't let my sisters know about this scheme either. To be revealed as a thief to my family was not an option.

After school, I sweated out waiting for my sisters to be out doing chores and for Mom and Dad to be in the barn. I slipped into their bedroom closet. The mingled smell of tobacco and cigarette smoke, sweat and a tinge of cow manure that filled the closet surrounded me with a familiar and loved "Dad smell." But with the guilt of being a thief on my heart, I could hardly bear it. I listened for any sound that would say my sisters were back in the house. Hearing only silence, I slipped my hand into the trouser pocket.

Bonanza! There was a lot of change. I took a handful and sorted out a quarter, a nickel, a dime and a few pennies. I could get away with that, I thought. And it would keep Virtus at bay. I put the rest of the change back in Dad's pocket; made sure everything was hanging just as before and backed out of the closet. My knees felt all rubbery, my guts turned loose and dangerously watery.

The next day Virtus was waiting for me the second I stepped down from the stile. My skin burned as I handed over the money.

He looked at the little pile of change and growled as mean as the neighbor dog, "That's not enough."

"It's all I could get," I whispered, near tears. "I'll get more tomorrow."

Telling my sisters, telling my parents, telling Miss Fowler never came to my mind as a viable option. I set aside "Thou Shalt Not Steal" from Sunday School. I trashed

"Honor Thy Father." I gave up on the ability to look at my own sorry face in the mirror. Keeping my word and paying my debt to Virtus seemed like the only things that mattered.

That night I repeated my burglar routine. And the next night. And the next night. Each day I handed over a small payment on my million-dollar bet. Each night I suffered a stomachache of guilt and regret.

Within a week guilt weighed more heavily on me than the possibility I would be found out. I couldn't make myself go into Dad's closet again. I didn't sleep that night, thinking of the disaster that waited me when I didn't hand over the payment to Virtus the next morning. I didn't care. I didn't know what would happen when Dad and Mom and my sisters and Miss Fowler found out, but I guessed I'd just have to live with it.

I dragged my feet all the way to school the next day. I climbed the stile like a convicted man going to the gallows. Virtus didn't wait until I was in the schoolyard.

"Where's my money?" he barked.

"I don't have it. I can't get it." My throat closed up on the words. Humiliation burned red on my face. I couldn't look Virtus in the eyes.

"You have to. You owe me," he demanded, his dirty hand palm up in front of me, his eyes black as a thunderstorm.

"I can't. I just can't," I whimpered. Tears filled my eyes and I swiped them away with the back of my hand.

"Humph!" he growled. "Guess I can't trust you." Virtus glared at me for one thousand-year-long second, turned on his heel and stomped away.

That was it? He wasn't going to tell? I could not

believe it. As quickly as the threat was there, it was gone. Within a few days, we were having lunch together again under the box elder trees, playing catch, running foot races around the school.

In the course of the week, I'd paid off roughly $2 of my million-buck bet. With those $2 went more than a pound of self-respect. Though my parents, my sisters and Miss Fowler never found out about my step across the line into theft, dishonor and shame, the scars were indelible. I never bet a million bucks again, nor a hundred, nor any amount I was not prepared to pay on the spot with cash of my own.

Irving and Virtus didn't stay with us for a whole year. Their family moved on. My sister Jane recalls them as "nice fellows," dirt notwithstanding. Virtus wrote a letter to me once after they were gone. He signed it "your friend."

Laundry Lessons

"We have to try it again. Here's another shirt," Jane said as she plucked one of Dad's blue work shirts out of a plastic bag full of shirts—clean, sprinkled and rolled—all ready to iron. "Start with the yoke," she directed.

I grabbed the damp shirt out of her hand and flopped it onto the ironing board. "I know where to start," I huffed. I knew to start with the yoke, then iron the collar, then the left sleeve and cuff, front and back, then the right sleeve and cuff, front and back, then the right front, taking particular care around the buttons, then the back below the yoke, and finally the left front, again taking care with the button hole placket where it was so easy to iron in wrinkles. I knew all this and I was tired of practicing.

Recoiling, Jane threw up her hands. "Don't get mad at me. We have to get this perfect."

"I know," I sighed, contrite as I smoothed the shirt out on the silver ironing board cover and picked up the heavy iron. "Let's go through what we're going to say again."

"Okay," Jane said. "Let's start." With that, we both stood straighter, mustered bright smiles to our faces, and

133

beamed at our audience: Mom who stood with her back toward us as she fixed dinner, and Sue, who was lying on the floor with one arm over the dog, balancing the book she was reading on her chest. Sitting at the table with a pan wedged between her knees and a knife in her hands as she peeled potatoes, Grandma was the only one paying Jane and me the least attention.

"Today we will show you the proper way to iron a shirt and fold it to store in a drawer or to pack in a suitcase," Jane said.

Picking up our planned patter and making eye contact with the audience as we'd been taught, I said, "We start by ironing the yoke and collar." Then, as Jane described step-by-step what I was doing, I ironed the yoke and collar before moving on to the sleeves.

When our county extension agent, Mrs. Ruth, came to our last 4-H meeting to teach all of us to iron shirts, she suggested that ironing a shirt would be a good team demonstration for the county fair. Jane had looked at me just as I looked at her. What a good idea! Both of us dreamed of doing so well at the county level that we would be selected to take our demonstration to the state fair in Des Moines. The dream was enough to lure us into preparing a demonstration every year. Success had eluded us so far, but this was another chance.

4-H programming cycled through the home and garden arts, each year focusing on a different skill set we needed to master before we married and set up our own homes—gardening and canning, home decorating, sewing, cooking. Each club member chose individual projects to demonstrate mastery of what we learned. We entered the best of our efforts into the county fair. Some projects were 'once and done.' You couldn't refinish a table more than once, for instance. Others we did over and over. Sue made so many batches of chocolate chip cookies one year Dad took to calling them 'rabbit turd cookies,' and though he never met a cookie he didn't like, he never again picked up a chocolate chip cookie with much enthusiasm.

Jane and I often partnered for team demonstrations. Two years older than I, Jane was capable of more complicated projects but she teamed up with me because it was more convenient than getting together with another club member who might live miles away. Plus I wasn't totally incapable of learning, and Mom probably made her.

We launched into the shirt ironing project with enthusiasm. That enthusiasm was soon lost in the repetition of preparation. We had practiced our demonstration on six shirts already that day. The biggest challenge came in folding the shirt. The reality was that we never folded shirts at our house. Hung on hangers, the top button secured so the fronts didn't sag and rewrinkle, shirts lined the closet rods. None filled dresser drawers, and virtually the only vacations we ever took were day trips to visit relatives. Even when we went to Wisconsin to visit our relatives on Dad's side for a confirmation, a wedding or a funeral, we left the farm after the cows were milked in the morning and got back before they had to be milked at night. Packing a shirt just wasn't necessary.

Who knows why we chose to fold the shirt for this demonstration. Maybe we dreamed of taking a vacation someday that was longer than a day. Maybe we imagined packing our future husbands' shirts for a vacation or business trip. Maybe we came away from Mrs. Ruth's suggestion thinking it was something we had to do. Maybe we thought it was an added challenge to the demonstration, successful completion of which would push us over the top in the judges' eyes and the state fair trip would certainly be ours. For whatever reason, folding the shirt was an element of our demonstration and we kept at it, no matter how vexing.

We had learned to iron using handkerchiefs and dish towels, expanded our skills as we pressed open seams for sewing projects, and now sought to perfect the art on Dad's shirts. There were plenty of opportunities to practice. Every week there was a basket of ironing that came out of the week's laundry.

Laundry began on Saturday when we stripped the sheets off our beds, gathered up bath and kitchen towels, and retrieved socks and underwear from the back of our closets and under the bed, throwing it all down the laundry chute by the bathroom door. We kids made up our own beds, pulling the fresh sheets out from between the mattress and springs where Mom put them after they were washed and dried so the replacements were handy when it came time to repeat the chore the next Saturday.

On Monday, Mom pulled the wringer washer and rinse tubs out into the middle of the basement, sorted the laundry into piles, and worked her way through load after load.

As my sisters and I grew older, we helped with the laundry but only with hanging clothes up, not with the actual washing. I wanted to help wash the clothes, but Mom said, 'No.' She told the story I'd heard a gazillion times about Grandma getting her arm caught in the wringer. Wide-eyed, with goose bumps prickling my arms, I shuddered, "Ewww! How did she get it out?"

"She hit this release button." To demonstrate, Mom banged the release and the two rollers flew apart. "You have to be careful when you feed clothes through the wringer not to get your arm caught." Even when she let me feed a pair of pants or a shirt into the wringer, she watched the entire time. The release button was also banged when too much cloth fed through and choked the wringer, a problem an inexperienced kid could make happen with relative frequency, particularly when it came to Dad's heavy denim work pants.

It fascinated me when Mom banged the release and the rollers flew apart. Each time I imagined it was my arm and I wondered how it felt to have your arm flattened between those hard, black rollers. Would my arm look like Wile E. Coyote after he was run over by a truck? Would my arm pop back to its original shape moments later?

The story about Grandma's arm in the wringer was only slightly less horrifying than the story about Grandma when she became distracted one day as she worked at the sewing machine and stitched right through her finger. Apparently Mom thought I could not be careful enough, because she never let me do the washing. I did not, however, escape the sewing machine, where I learned to create all of my clothes except for underwear. And I did not escape hanging up clothes or bringing them in from the line after they dried.

In the winter, Mom hung everything from white sheets to Dad's heavy denim work pants on the lines that stretched between the rafters in the basement. The effect was that of a maze of clothes with a smell that mingled damp clean with wood smoke from the furnace.

When I was little, my sisters and I rode our tricycles 'round and round' the stove and in and out of the piles of laundry. If Butch wasn't outside with Dad, he chased around the stove after us, barking until Mom told him to be quiet. Then he nosed at each pile of clothes, as though checking to see that all family members were accounted for, circled around three times and lay down next to the furnace where pretty soon he'd be asleep, his feet twitching from time to time as he chased rabbits or cats or cows in his dreams.

In the summertime, we hung laundry on the clothesline in the backyard. When I was tall enough to reach the clotheslines—maybe when I was about 10—Mom pressed me into service lugging heaping baskets of clean, wet clothes upstairs to the clothesline. Before hanging up a single item, I wiped each line clean with the rag stuffed in the corner of the clothespin bag. It was easiest to reach the center of the line and that's where I began hanging clothes, counting on their weight to pull the rest of the line down far enough that I could reach it.

Each item had its own proper way to hang, a way I learned from watching Mom. Matching the seams to create a crease as they dried, I hung Dad's work pants with one leg clipped to one line and the other leg clipped to a parallel line. Shirts hung upside down, clipped at the side seams, sleeves hanging toward the ground like so many kids hanging by their knees from the jungle gym. Displaying our underwear where hired men or visitors driving in our lane might see them embarrassed me, so I made sure to hang these items on the lines between the sheets and shirts.

Hanging up laundry was not my favorite thing to do. The damp sheets were cold and clammy when they flapped in the breeze against my back and legs as I hung more clothes on the next line. Still, after I clipped the last sock out of the last basket onto the only remaining two inches of clothesline, I had to admit the result looked pretty good. And when I went to bed between clean sheets, I slept with dreams drenched in sunshine and fresh air.

When the laundry was dry, we folded it as it came off the line. Baskets of laundry disappeared into dressers and closets at the end of the day. In those days before permanent press, much of the laundry was ironed before we put it away. Since this was also before steam irons, all that laundry had to be sprinkled before we took to it with a hot iron.

For sprinkling, Mom took out a little aluminum pan, filled it with cold water and with her finger tips flicked drops of water onto the shirts, hankies, dish towels and pillow cases she rolled up and put back in the laundry basket to be ironed on Tuesday. If Mom thought there was any chance the damp clothes would mildew, she put the sprinkled clothes in a big plastic bag and stowed it in the refrigerator until she was ready to iron.

On Tuesday Mom setup the ironing board in the kitchen, brought out the basket of damp clothes, and everything from hankies to shirts became wrinkle-free under the heavy iron. As soon as she was confident we would not burn ourselves or the clothes, Mom began our ironing education on her dainty hankies and Dad's rugged farmer handkerchiefs.

Tidy stacks of pretty, floral hankies with scalloped edges filled a corner of Mom's top dresser drawer. She always had one or two fresh hankies in her purse and as we grew older, hankies were tucked into our purses before we went to church or out on dates. Dad used a multitude of handkerchiefs each week. Red or blue paisley print handkerchiefs large enough to serve as a scarf on my head were standard in his work pants pocket. More refined, white cotton squares, some sporting his initials embroidered in the corner, replaced those hardworking squares when he dressed up for church, weddings or funerals. Because we all used so many, hankies and handkerchiefs were an excellent choice for Christmas presents.

Ironing hankies, removing all the wrinkles, folding them neatly in half and then thirds, ironing each fold into a sharp crease, creating a neat stack to go back in the dresser drawers was like giving a little gift each week to the person who would use them.

When Grandma Jensen came to stay with us, which she did every summer, she took over the ironing chores. She ironed hankies, too, but not her own. Each night, she washed her hanky in the bathroom sink and plastered it on the screen of the bedroom window to dry.

In the morning, Grandma donned one of the cotton shirtwaist dresses she wore every day. She pulled on nylons, rolling them down to just above her knees, and covered her pure white hair with a silver net. Finally, she plucked the now-dry hanky from the window screen, folded it and put it in her pocket.

When Jane and I took on the 4-H shirt ironing demonstration—and for one summer claimed squatter's rights at the ironing board—I can only imagine what Grandma thought.

As tedious as the hours of ironing could be, they were also the hours when Grandma watched 'her shows' as Mom always called the soaps.

A dedicated follower of the perpetual heartaches and never-ending trials of *Search for Tomorrow, Guiding Light* and *As the World Turns*, Grandma set the ironing board up in front of the TV in the living room. Piece by piece, she drew shirts and pillowcases and hankies and dresses from the laundry basket, stretched them on the ironing board, flicked water with her fingertips and eliminated wrinkles in our clothes while the characters in her dramas solved the problems in their lives. Every week the basket of ironing was full again with the same laundry; every week the soaps offered the same problems to be solved. Because of Grandma, the hopelessness of soap operas and the never-ending challenge of laundry are tied together forever in my mind.

Grandma had her own way to iron. She could have taught Jane and me a lot about ironing had we asked her. But we didn't ask. And she didn't offer. That summer, in one swoop, we commandeered both her job and her reason to spend time in front of the TV.

As we practiced, shirt after shirt crossed the ironing board. Either Jane or I could have ironed a shirt flawlessly in our sleep. After each shirt was ironed, we folded it, oh so carefully, smoothing each crease until our shirts looked just like the ones we saw in stores. We practiced what we would say and how we would stand until I could do Jane's part of the demonstration, she could do mine.

Beyond teaching the basic skills, 4-H was designed to mold each of us into confident presenters and leaders. Along the way we learned other lessons. Unintended lessons.

One year, I tackled bread baking. Mom baked six big loaves of white bread every week and I expect it was no accident it came out of the oven and was set to cool on the bread board under a white cotton dish towel just before we walked in the door, home from school. The warm, yeasty smell of just-baked bread drifted out of the house and drew us in as irresistibly as if we were hummingbirds seeking the nectar in red flowers.

"I get the heel," I shouted. Mom sliced off an inch-thick heel. "I get the other one," Sue said. Without ceremony, Mom turned the loaf around and sliced off the other end. It never bothered Jane to take the next slice in. Mom put the butter dish and knives on the table and we sat, slathering on butter that melted at once into the warm bread, eating slice after slice and spilling the adventures of the day.

Homemade bread was on the table for every meal.

Dad expected it. Mom complied. It stood to reason that learning to bake bread would be a 4-H goal. White bread was the staple but during that year, I launched into the world of bread forms that never made it to our table at any other time.

Dinner rolls. German black bread. Sweet breads like Martha Washington's Fan that used maraschino cherries to dot the blades. Crusty French bread. Breads in all shapes, flavors and colors lined our cupboards that year. I never tired of kneading flour into dough, smelling fresh-baked bread throughout the house, slicing into a loaf to see a perfect texture.

That year, Jane and I prepared a team demonstration on bread baking for the county fair. By that time, I was ever so conscious of makeup and jewelry, wearing two or three rings at a time, on each hand. We prepared for our presentation so carefully: our uniforms spotless; our hair carefully combed and held away from our faces with barrettes; our utensils and ingredients in place. Our demonstration was going well.

Standing behind the table on the elevated demonstration platform in the fairgrounds 4-H building with rows of spectators seated on folding chairs in front of us, and the judges dead center in the front row, Jane mixed all the ingredients while I explained quantities and steps. When it was time to knead the dough, we executed a flawless exchange of responsibility. Jane took over talking as I sprinkled flour on the board, turned out the dough, dusted flour on my hands and began to knead. Only then, with my hands deep in the stickiest moment of bread making, did I realize I had not taken off my rings. Dough globbed around and under each ring.

I glanced at Jane. She saw my error. I hesitated for half a breath but continued to knead, hoping no one in the audience, particularly the judges, would see. They were, after all, several feet away. It was possible. But just then, I heard a girl say—in a stage whisper just loud enough for everyone to hear—"Oh, she should have taken off her rings." I was mortified. When I was finished kneading, I wiped my hands as well as I could, pretending all the while the rings did not exist, even as I picked up the talking part of the presentation as Jane formed the loaves into pans.

We finished the presentation as we began—flawlessly. There was only that one little thing with the rings. I was kicking myself when we read the judge's note, 'Should have removed rings before demonstration!!!'

Whether it was the rings that kept us from being chosen for the state fair that year, I do not know. But it didn't matter all that much. At the end of the year, I received the 4-H Bread Baking pin, the award I coveted and wore with a shameless amount of pride on the collar of my uniform.

Now we had another chance at the state fair trip. Ironing and folding a shirt. We practiced. Oh, how we practiced. And we had it nailed. We were certain we had it nailed.

The night before, we ironed our uniforms and hung them neatly on hangers to be donned just before we presented. We would be at the fair all day and could not risk ketchup drips or cotton candy smears. The morning of the demonstration, Jane and I raced through the barn chores. We checked the shirts we had sprinkled the night before and stored in the refrigerator. We gathered everything we needed: iron, ironing board, hangers (even though the shirt would be folded), and the shirts and put everything in the car. We were r-e-a-d-y.

We watched a few of the other demonstrations,

decided we were every bit as good as they were, and took a walk until it was our turn. When we stepped on to the demonstration stage, we were calm. The presentation went just as we had practiced it. Neither of us missed a line. Neither of us made a mistake in the ironing. When we were finished folding the shirt, we presented it with pride at the judges' table.

"Very nice," one judge said with a warm smile as she took the shirt from Jane's hands.

"Thank you," Jane and I said in unison.

"Yes, it is, isn't it?" the second judge nodded as she began to unfold the shirt. We beamed.

"Oh," the second judge said. She glanced at the first judge.

Oh, what? Anxiety snaked through my calm confidence. I looked at Jane, who cocked an eyebrow in question.

"You see there's a wrinkle in the fold," the second judge explained, pointing to a small rumple in the fabric where the sleeve folded in at the elbow.

"A wrinkle in the fold . . ." I repeated, my voice trailing off as I saw the smallest of wrinkles. Such a small wrinkle. It could not be that important.

"But the rest of it is perfect," Jane spoke to defend our work.

"Yes, it would have been perfect without this wrinkle," the judge persisted. "I'm afraid we have to give you a red ribbon."

A flush rose up Jane's neck. I stared at the judges gape-mouthed. Not only not good enough for the state fair, but not good enough for even a first-place blue ribbon. Defeat must have been written across our faces in a red to match the offending second-place ribbon because the first judge, the infinitely kinder judge, added in a half-apology, "If you had just hung the shirt up instead of folding it, then it would have been a blue."

As we accepted our now unfolded and deplorably wrinkled shirt out of the judges' hands, we thought to mumble 'thank you' before we escaped backstage.

"*There's this one little wrinkle so we have to give you a red ribbon*," Jane parroted as she flung the offending shirt on a chair and fought back tears.

"We practiced so much. We did the best we could," I whimpered, slumped on a chair, head in my hands.

"Let's change and get out of here," Jane said. "I can't bear to hear any more." I nodded.

We stripped out of our uniforms and jammed everything we'd brought into the trunk of the car in a huff, hurt giving way to anger as we continued to smart from the disappointment.

"We did a harder project," I said, kicking a clod of dirt across the road. "Wouldn't you think that would count for something?"

"I bet those girls from Maquoketa win again," Jane speculated. "They always win."

Back and forth we ranted until we worked through all our hurt, all our anger. Take the easy way out and get a first-place ribbon. Or do a harder task and be rewarded with a red ribbon. I thought about that for quite some time.

Looking back on those experiences, I realize that 4-H taught us many things and I have to say most of the lessons fell into the asset column. I used the presentation skills I learned throughout a long career in public relations. I still take pride in a freshly baked loaf of bread, and I don't take off my wedding ring to knead the dough. I can iron a shirt perfectly to this day though I will occasionally find a wrinkle when unfolding one out of my suitcase. And I still think the judges were unfair with their judging. But then that's a good lesson, too. Life isn't always fair.

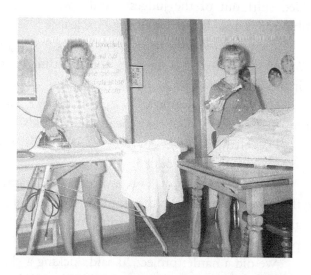

Another Cow Story

The screen door slammed and I was yanked out of the book I was reading by the sound of Dad's heavy boots clomping across the kitchen linoleum. Though Mom was working at the sink, he said nothing to her. Instead, Dad walked directly to the phone, pulled out a chair and sat while he thumbed through the pages of the phone book.

The thick whir-click sound as Dad dialed each number on the heavy black desk phone echoed in the quiet air of the kitchen. Dad didn't use the phone for casual purposes. When he left the house after breakfast, he might not come in again until dinner time at noon. The sound of his footsteps. The hum, click of the dial phone. I broke from reading and listened. Who was he calling? Why?

"Yeah. I got a cow down with milk fever," Dad said without even saying hello to the person at the other end. "How soon can Doc get out here?"

Dad wasn't joking with the person on the phone like he usually did, and the worry in his voice sent a chill up my back. If a cow came down with milk fever, it was usually within days after she calved. The cow lay down, her head turned unnaturally back across her stomach, and she didn't get up. I didn't know much about milk fever but I did know it could kill the cow if it wasn't treated fast.

"Where is she?" Mom asked after Dad hung up. The concern in her voice raised goose bumps on my arms. Raised in town, Mom visited her uncles' farms when she was growing up, but her first real experience with farming came when Dad got out of the Army and they moved to this farmstead. They'd milked cows from the beginning. The cows were our livelihood; the monthly milk check paid all the bills. When a cow was sick, Mom knew Dad would be more on edge, tense, curt. Try as she might to be supportive, Dad kept his worries to himself, believing perhaps that this was the man's job, that a woman couldn't understand, that a 'town girl,' even after all these years on the farm, wouldn't be much use when it came to this.

"Down the lane," Dad said as he headed out the door. "I'm going down to try to get her up. Send Doc down when he gets here."

I bolted from the couch and raced after him. "Which cow is it?" I asked, taking two steps to every one of his. I couldn't help but think about the cow and calf we brought up from the pasture that spring. "Is she going to be okay?"

"It's 15," he said, glancing down at me. "I don't know if she'll be okay. She didn't eat all her feed when we milked last night. Then she didn't come up to the yard this morning."

Dad strode through the barn, across the barnyard, wasting no time with the calves or cats, moving with an uncharacteristic urgency that filled me with anxiety. The morning sun was already warm, burning the dew off the grass. It would be a hot day. As we left the barnyard, I spotted the cow lying in a gully at the bottom of the lane.

Rutted with cow paths formed as the cows filed back and forth daily from barnyard to pasture and back again, the lane was dusty, the dust interrupted by an occasional weed that escaped the cows' hooves. I placed my feet in the ruts worn by the cows as they walked single file, the lead cow taking the easiest route, the rest following. No doubt this cow lagged behind, already suffering from the onset of milk fever, then lying down when her legs gave out, unable to carry her farther.

Dad crouched by the cow's head, ran his hand along her shoulder, looked into her listless eyes and said to me, "Let's get her up. We have to get her to the barn." When he stood and moved to her back quarters, the ache that had formed in my stomach unclenched a little. Doing something felt better than doing nothing.

"Get behind her shoulders and push when I do," he said. Positioning his strong hands under the cow's hip, Dad leaned all his weight into lifting. I braced my skinny legs against the rise of one of the cow paths and leaned against the uphill side of the cow's shoulder. Together we pushed with all our might. Dad's muscles rippled, sweat formed on his forehead and trickled down his neck. Sweat already soaked through his shirt. In response to all our effort, the cow groaned out a low bellow, but barely moved.

Dad grabbed the cow's tail and twisted it. That should have made her move. But it didn't. I felt a frightening urgency in my chest and leaned into the cow's shoulder determined to be useful, to show Dad I could help. We pushed again, giving it everything we had. The cow heaved forward but fell back as soon as we let up, and a sigh escaped her that sounded like the moaning of wind through the pine trees back of our house in the night. We couldn't move a cow that didn't want to move. I don't know why I was crying all of a sudden. I brushed away the tears with the back of my arm, pretending sweat was dripping on my face, so that Dad didn't see.

Dad stepped back and surveyed the cow. "Damn it, I should have kept her in last night," he rumbled as he pulled a blue handkerchief from his back pocket and wiped away the sweat streaming down his face and neck. I squinted into the sun, watching Dad's face. I didn't say anything. He seemed mad at the cow, mad at me, mad at himself.

"Stay here, Squirt," he said. "I'm going to get the tractor. Maybe we can lift her with the loader."

I watched him trudge back up the lane, resolve in the stiffness of his back and the speed with which he moved. He didn't say it. He didn't have to. I knew how important this cow was, how important each cow was. I sat down, cross-legged in the dust by the cow's head, my back to the sun. I studied the way her head drew oddly back against her side. Milk fever made them do that. I didn't know why.

I stroked the cow's neck, scratched behind her ears, talked to her. "You'll be okay, girl. Dad will get you up. Don't you worry." I got up and pulled a couple of handfuls of grass from the fence row, thinking if she ate something maybe she'd feel like walking. "Here you go, girl, some nice grass," I urged. "Try this, I bet you'll like it." The cow showed no interest in the fresh, green grass held right under her nose; she didn't take even a nibble. I sat back down in the dust, helpless, stroking her neck, brushing away the flies that gathered around her eyes, smoothing the fine gray dust off her black-and-white sides.

In minutes, I heard the engine of the tractor cough and sputter into an even rhythm and saw Dad negotiate the Farmall M through the gate and down the lane. The tractor was already fitted with the loader because Dad had been hauling manure this week, clearing away the pile that grew by the day as we cleaned the barn after every milking. I saw the vet standing on the toolbar, gripping the seat with one hand and his bag with the other. He came whenever Dad called, because Dad didn't call for the vet unless he needed him. Now. They climbed down from the tractor. Dad set a bucket of water he brought near the cow but she showed no more interest in the water than she had in my handful of grass.

A tall, slender man with square shoulders, strong arms, a thick thatch of unruly grey hair and legs so bowed he rocked when he walked, Doc didn't waste time. He bent down by the cow, smoothing his hand over her stomach. "How long has she been down," he asked.

"She didn't come up to milk last night."

"I tried to get her to eat some grass," I offered, feeling a little bit important to have been left with the cow, to be here along with Dad, talking with the vet. "She wouldn't take any."

"No, I suppose not." Doc offered a half smile then turned to look in the cow's eyes. He moved around and took the cow's temperature by putting a thermometer in her butt. Embarrassed, I looked at my feet, scuffed my toe in the dust, until he finished.

"She's been a good cow. Can we save her?" Dad asked.

"It's a tough one," Doc replied. "Once they go down, if we don't treat them fast enough, there's not much we can do."

"What if we get her up?" Dad asked.

"Her legs just won't hold her. Even if you could get her up the lane, she'd just go down in the yard." Doc was

151

patient, but realistic. "I can give her a shot and see if it helps, but I'm not optimistic."

"Do it," Dad said, his voice flat.

Doc got the syringe and a medicine bottle out of his bag, upended the bottle, inserted the needle, and drew the solution in until the syringe was full. He held the syringe up toward the sun, tapped it lightly with one finger and depressed the plunger until a few drops squirted out of the needle along with tiny air bubbles. "How many lactations?" he asked as he found a vein and emptied the syringe.

"Five. She's a good producer. Had a heifer calf day before yesterday."

Pride in this cow hung on Dad's words but there was no smile on his face. He wasn't joking with Doc; they weren't talking about the crops or what was going on in town like they usually did. Five lactations meant the cow was about seven years old. Not young, but she could be a good producer for a few more years yet. In her prime. The clench came back in my stomach.

"We'll see if this helps." Doc knelt to close up his bag. "Call me if you see any change."

"I'll do that," Dad said as he took off his cap and wiped his head again with the handkerchief. "Damn, it's hot," he said. He looked past the cow, out across the cornfields where heat shimmered visibly above the corn tassels. When he changed the subject, it was as though he was letting go of the cow in some meaningful way, balancing hope with reality, acknowledging that she might not be saved.

I looked up at Dad and swallowed hard, an aching hollowness in my chest.

"We'll give you a ride back up to the yard, Doc," Dad said, as he climbed onto the tractor seat. "C'mon

Squirt. We can't do anything else right now. She's got water and grass. We'll come back down after dinner."

I crouched down beside the cow one last time and smoothed the hair on her forehead. Whispered to her, "We'll be back." Then I climbed up beside Dad and perched on the wheel guard, one hand on the guard, one hand on the bar holding the headlamps, hanging on tight for the bumpy ride back up the lane. Doc stood behind Dad on the toolbar.

The sun was high in the cloudless, blue sky. It was coming on noon and the light threw flat, harsh shadows. Dad and Doc exchanged few words over the noise of the tractor. I watched the cow as long as I could see her, and then she was gone.

Economics 101

"I don't want to," I whined, shifting from foot to foot and all but stamping the floor as I stood hunched over the sink.

"Those radishes are beautiful," Mom exclaimed with a bright smile, ignoring my tone. Peering over my shoulder at the sink full of radishes I'd pulled from my garden plot that morning, she added, "It won't be so bad, you'll see." Mom approached every chore as if there were nothing she'd rather be doing and she swept us along in her wake. Usually.

"I still don't want to." My whine turned to a pout.

"Well, you need to. It's part of the project. So you may as well get it done." Mom's tone let me know she'd heard about all the whining she was going to. After planting a reassuring pat on my shoulder, she turned to rolling out pie crusts.

Slowly, methodically, I stuck each radish under the flood of cold water pouring out of the tap, determined that if I had to do this chore, at least I wasn't going to do it fast. And I wasn't going to enjoy it.

Earlier that spring all three of us decided to take on

a 4-H garden project, so after Dad plowed up the 40– by 300–foot area that constituted the family garden, Mom helped us measure off plots for our projects.

From the time I was two, I'd helped plant potatoes, carrying my little pail of seed potato sections, walking next to Dad as he worked his way down the row. Each time he stepped firmly on the spade, slicing the ground, leaning forward on the shovel handle to pry the soil open a few inches, I bent down and slid a wrinkly section of potato deep into the hole, the 'eye' pointing up as the ground closed around it. Back and forth we went, row after row, planting enough to yield bushels of potatoes, enough potatoes to fill the bin in the fruit cellar, enough to last a year.

Each year as we grew older, my sisters and I were entrusted with smaller and smaller seeds, progressing from individual potato pieces the size of our little fists, to dropping three sweet corn kernels in each hole, to spacing shriveled lima beans and peas three inches apart in a trench, to filtering the smallest carrot and radish seeds along a shallow furrow. Each day after we planted the garden, we knelt on the sofa looking out the living room picture window, watching for the first hint of rows to validate our efforts. Anxiety ran rampant when the skies turned black and torrential spring rains threatened to flood out the rows. Hope returned when the sun shone again and tender shoots poked up through the mud.

As the summer wore on, our enthusiasm was tempered by the heat of the sun and the constant challenge of weeds. At the least little sign we didn't have something to do, Mom offered up, "Go hoe the garden."

The enthusiasm I'd felt for my 4-H project ran just this course. Meticulously, I'd measured out the rows, dragged the hoe to create furrows, dropped in seeds and tamped the soil firmly over them. "Am I doing this right?" I asked Mom before and after each row. She coached me at each step—"That's just right," or "Plant those seeds two inches apart," or "Just feather the dirt with your hand to cover those carrot seeds"—as I crawled on hands and knees back and forth between the rows. At the end of each row, I stabbed a twig upright so I could tell where I'd been. When the seed packet was empty, I stuck it on the twig, a colorful flag reminder of what was planted in the row. I devoted the 10 x 15-foot space of my garden to radishes, carrots, lettuce, onions, peas and green beans, leaving space-eating plants like tomatoes, potatoes and sweet corn to the big garden.

With a sense of importance akin to what I imagined Dad felt when he did the farm records, I spread open the fresh, unmarked pages of my 4-H record book on the kitchen table. In neat little rows marred only by my hopelessly sloppy handwriting, I recorded the cost of seed bought in bulk at the Feed & Grain in Maquoketa, the dates of planting, the dates it rained, the dates to germination, the dates of harvesting, transcribing each entry in pencil and later re-creating the record in ink to take to the county fair.

What I had acknowledged only briefly and just as quickly dismissed at the start of the project, was the requirement that I sell some of the produce and calculate how much my garden would return on the investment if I sold everything. I could not fathom the face-to-face transaction required to sell my vegetables. The very idea of approaching someone, anyone, and asking if they wanted to buy something caused my stomach to go weak.

Each day as I walked the rows of my garden plot, watching the vegetables mature, I was alternately excited by the progress and faintly dreading the inevitable. There was little joy that morning as I washed the bright red radishes and rinsed the green tops. As clods of dirt clinging to the radishes turned to mud and trailed through my fingers and down the drain, I agonized.

"Maybe I could do it this afternoon?" I threw out a brilliant delaying tactic.

"No, you go this morning. I bet Edna would love to have fresh radishes for dinner." Grabbing the dishrag, Mom wiped the flour off her hands, rummaged through the junk drawer next to the refrigerator and pulled out some rubber bands. "Here. Bunch them up with these," she said.

Last time we were in town, I'd looked at radishes in the grocery store and saw they tied 10 in a bunch and sold the bunch for 15 cents. I tied up 12 radishes in each bunch, planning to sell them for 5 cents. As I looked at the still-wet, bundled radishes heaped on the drain board by the sink, I admitted to myself they did look pretty. Better even than those in the store. Still, I couldn't get excited about selling them.

"But why would she want these radishes?" I persisted. "She has a garden. I bet she doesn't even want any radishes."

"I don't think hers are ready yet. You had your garden in early. Now get going. And hurry back. We have to get dinner on the table."

Scooping up the three bunches of radishes, I headed out the door. Mom had given me the choice of trying to sell the radishes to strangers in town or to our neighbors. I'd agonized over which would be worse, going to someone I didn't know and being rejected or going to someone I did know and being rejected. Rejection was really the only possible outcome of trying to sell produce in a farm community like ours where gardens and fresh produce were as plentiful as the stars in the sky on a clear night. I decided being rejected close to home was maybe a little bit less horrible.

The lane from the highway to our house was on the property line between our farm and Miller's. The lane split by the mailboxes at the top of the hill with half the lane coming into our place and the other half going to Miller's. Edna and Bill were our closest neighbors in terms of distance and we neighbored back and forth. On May Day we fixed little baskets out of construction paper and filled them with violets to sneak over and hang on Edna's door. She surprised us one year with a banana cream pie made with a vanilla wafer crust and topped with whipped cream. When our lilac bush was in full bloom, we always took Edna a bouquet. Dad and Bill agreed on who would do what and when on the fences that divided our fields. But since Millers didn't have kids my age, when I did go there, it was usually trailing Mom.

With gray hair combed neatly in a roll that ringed her head and an apron protecting her ample waist, Edna reminded me of my Grandma Denter, a woman who always smiled and was not in the least scary. But she was still totally intimidating because she was an adult and I had to try to sell her something I was absolutely, positively certain she did not want.

As I dragged my leaden feet toward my first sales call, I stopped by my garden plot and considered how many other bunches of radishes were yet to be picked. Scuffing my bare toes in the dust, I sighed. The 4-H requirement was to sell all of one crop. I sighed again and groaned. At this point, I could not work up the energy to be grateful I did not also have to sell the carrots and onions and lettuce and peas and beans.

I trudged on, all the while rehearsing what I would

say. Just past the mailboxes, I stopped. My legs and feet had begun to feel as heavy as blocks of cement. I looked back at our house and considered whether I could just go back and tell Mom Edna wasn't home. My skin prickled with nerves. I looked toward Edna's house and wished their dog Berle would race at me so I could run away. A white German Shepherd-sized dog, Berle wasn't mean, but the way he and our dog Butch barked at each other, no one was ever completely sure. If Berle had run up to me, I could have turned back and Mom might have accepted that as a credible excuse. Looking around, I waited in momentary optimism for Berle to come around the barn. He didn't.

I sighed, swallowed and plodded the rest of the way to Edna's door. The sun was beating against my back when I knocked. For a split second I thought I might be lucky and she wouldn't be home. While this wasn't likely since Edna didn't drive and it was close to noon, a girl could hope. No luck. I heard Edna come through the kitchen. I stepped back off the cement step as she opened the door.

"Why, Carol. Hello." She glanced behind me, looking for Mom, and then turned a puzzled gaze to me.

Locking my knees and swallowing my reluctance, I opened my mouth and spilled everything I'd thought to say in one breathless rush: "Hello, Mrs. Miller. I wondered if you wanted to buy some radishes. There are 12 in a bunch. They are five cents."

Edna looked at me for a moment, clearly puzzled. "Why don't you come inside so I can get a look at what you have," she said at last, opening the door wider. I stepped into the cool, dark of her kitchen and we sat at the table.

"Now tell me again what you have. You were talking a little fast and I didn't catch it all," she said as she set a plate of sugar cookies on the table and sat down herself with a cup of coffee.

"Thank you," I said as I reached for a cookie. Between bites I explained about the radishes and my 4-H project. To my great astonishment, Edna bought all three bunches. She offered to buy more when I had them.

In about 10 minutes, I left with three nickels tight in my hand. "Thank you," I called over my shoulder. I'd already said "thank you," at least three times, grateful beyond belief not to have to go to another neighbor, or even door-to-door in town as Mom threatened I'd have to do next. I skipped all the way home, arriving breathless at the house to share my success with Mom.

"Good for you!" Mom exclaimed. "Now put the money in your bank so you don't lose it and come set the table."

"I'll be right back," I bubbled, the distress of making the sale forgotten. In my bedroom, I grabbed my bank and my savings passbook, tucked right under the bank, and bounced onto the bed where I pulled out the plug and dumped the money out onto the chenille bedspread. Adding money to my bank always began with counting every penny that was already there. One by one the coins stacked up until I had Seven Pennies, Nine Nickels (including the three from selling my radishes), Eight Dimes and Four Quarters. Two Dollars and Thirty-Two Cents. It was a fortune.

Flipping over on my back, I reverently opened the passbook and reviewed each entry, so tiny, so carefully scripted by the bank teller, entries recording each deposit, each addition of interest. I regarded the interest entries with total amazement. I did not deposit this interest money but there it was—a gift—swelling the balance.

The first conscious memory I have of money as

160

something to have and let go of was in church. I was three years old, sitting on Dad's lap. The minister finished the sermon and the ushers made their way down the aisle, handing the dark brown, wooden collection plates to the people sitting on the aisles. Each person dropped in an offering envelope or dollar bills and passed the plate on down the row.

As a plate came hand to hand toward us, Dad pressed a single penny into my palm, closing my fingers tightly around it. "Now, don't drop it," he cautioned in a whisper. "You put it in the plate when it gets to us," he instructed, his breath carrying the lingering smell of the cigarette he stubbed out between the car and the church.

I was excited to hold that penny. It was warm and shiny. When the collection plate reached us, I extended my arm, turned my hand over and dropped the penny on to the pile of offering envelopes, bills and change accumulating in the plate.

It was over so fast, the possessing of that penny and the relinquishing of it to the church. Money was not handed out freely in our family. We worked for every cent. We budgeted how it was spent. Along with my first weekly allowance of 10 cents came a lesson in budgeting. Mom sat all of us girls down at the kitchen table with a tablet and pencil. Each budget session emphasized the rules of 10 percent for savings and 10 percent for the church. What went into savings stayed there.

The 15 cents I had just earned through my own labor, by selling what I had raised, created a sense of accomplishment unlike any I'd felt before. It did not cross my mind that I would spend any of this money. My cousins bought comic books every week and while I was antsy to get my hands on their Superman comics when we visited,

I thought them unbelievably extravagant for spending their money that way. I would never part with my money for something so fleeting.

I rolled over on my side, propped my chin on my fists and looked at the tidy stacks of pennies, nickels, dimes and quarters. Two dollars and thirty-two cents. With this much money, I would most definitely make a trip to the bank at the end of the month when Mom went to town for groceries. With this much money to deposit, my balance would be nearly $30. With this much money, who knows what I would be able to do someday?

With my first successful sales call behind me, I pulled, washed and bound more radishes. The initial dread of selling the radishes was behind me; now I had my eye fixed on the money I could earn in selling my produce. Jane and Sue pulled radishes from their garden plots, too, and at one point we had too many for the kitchen sink and opted for the bathtub. The tub was half full. Of course, Edna could not take them all, though she never turned us away when we knocked on her door. So one day the three of us loaded our washed and bound bunches of radishes in the car and Mom dropped us off at the trailer court on the east edge of Maquoketa.

While Mom drove on into town to get groceries, we went door to door at the trailer court. Using the same approach I used when I knocked on Edna's door the first time, but making a real effort to overcome my nerves and speak more slowly, I walked to one trailer after another. I worked my way down one side of the street while Jane and Sue went to trailers along the other side. Nerves filled my stomach before I knocked on each door. Satisfaction replaced the nerves each time I secured coins in my pocket when I made a sale. Amazing to me, we sold every last bunch.

In the next month, the dimes, nickels and quarters from my radish sales swelled my balance by another One Dollar and Twenty-Five Cents. When the end of the month arrived, I opened my piggy bank again and counted out the money yet another time, stacking it into neat piles. I left the pennies behind, and stowed coins adding up to Three Dollars and Thirty-Five Cents deep in my pocket for the trip to town. I kept my hand in a tight fist around this treasure to make sure it didn't get lost. In my other hand, I clutched my savings passbook. During the ride to town, I imagined the new total after my latest deposit. The row of figures, each line containing a figure larger than the last, enchanted me. I dreamed about having enough to do something big. Like go to college.

Pushing through the heavy glass doors, I entered the Maquoketa State Savings Bank. The official coolness of the marble floors, the polished dark woodwork of the tellers' cages, and soaring high ceilings reduced my voice to a whisper more awe-inspired than one I used at the public library. One just did not talk loudly in a bank.

"I am here to make a deposit," I spoke with great solemnity as I reached up to slip the passbook and my money under the grill to the lady teller sitting on the other side.

"Well, you have quite a balance here," the teller said as she counted the money twice and made yet another exceedingly neat entry into my passbook.

"I know." I blushed with pride. "I sold my radishes."

One Christmas

"I asked Santa for a Roy Rogers and Trigger," I whispered in a conspiratorial tone to the kids crowded around the stove at the back of the schoolhouse. Just in from recess, we piled our snow-soaked mittens on the top of the stove to dry and held our chapped red fingers as close to the stove as we could. We could not tell at first whether our fingers were cold or hot; either way, they stung.

"What are you talking about?" Larry scoffed. "There ain't no Santa Claus." Larry rubbed his palms together and then slapped them against the red circles of cold on his freckled cheeks.

All talk stopped and I saw all the kids staring at Larry and me. Some of the kids laughed but their laughs hung hollow in the air like the steam that spiraled above the stove as bits of ice fell from the mittens and sizzled on the hot surface. The smell of scorching wool filled the room.

"There is, too," I sputtered. "You don't know anything." I looked around, searching the faces of the other kids for support.

"Ain't either. Is there, Dennis?" Larry asked, elbowing the boy next to him.

A thin boy with white blond hair, Dennis and his sisters lived across the highway from us. He and Larry were in the same grade, two years behind me. Both of them spent more time acting up than they did studying, causing Miss Fowler no end of frustration.

Dennis rubbed the spot on his arm where Larry elbowed him and hesitated, looking down at the floor and scuffing the toe of one worn brown shoe against the heel of the other. Anyone could see Dennis was reluctant to contradict Larry, but he couldn't lie either. Not on something like this. "There is," he mumbled at last, "Santa comes to our house."

"See, I told you so," I puffed. Looking around again at the other kids, I saw my sister Jane smile at me. Taking her smile for confirmation, I nodded my head with an emphatic "Humph" of triumph.

His black eyes blazing at his friend's betrayal, Larry shouted, "Ain't either. He never brings any presents to our house. My mom said he ain't real."

"I'm going to ask Miss Fowler," I said. Whirling around, my hands balled into fists, my chin thrust up with a determined tilt, I stomped to the front of the room where Miss Fowler sat at her desk grading papers from the morning classes.

"What's all this?" she asked, looking up as every single student in the school—all 15 of us—jostled for position around her desk.

"Larry says there isn't a Santa Claus," I blurted, my feet planted squarely, fists jammed on hips, determined to prove my point by sheer force of will. "There is, too, isn't there." I demanded more than questioned.

In a considered, slow sweep, Miss Fowler looked at each one of us crowding in around her. We ranged in age from 5 to 14 and Miss Fowler, though she had no children herself, stood as an authority, as the authority, we all respected in the absence of our parents.

Taking off her wire-rimmed glasses, Miss Fowler rubbed her eyes for a second, tucked a strand of gray hair behind her ear, and settled the glasses back on her nose. "Well, of course there's a Santa Claus," she said in an even tone that could leave no doubt.

Grinning, I looked at Larry in triumph as the tension drained out of my stance.

Miss Fowler looked again at each of us individually. "It might be a good idea for each of you to talk with your parents about Santa if you have questions," she suggested.

Larry frowned. It was clear that he was mad. I didn't rub it in, but I didn't bother to hide my gloating, either.

With the skill of someone who had diffused many playground tussles, Miss Fowler diverted our attention. "I am glad you all are gathered here, now. Let's see who's ready to recite their part in the Christmas program. Who wants to go first?"

Hands shot into the air. "Let me. Let me. Let me!" I hopped from one foot to the other. I was oh-so-ready to recite my poem.

I might talk with Mom about Santa, I thought, but then I didn't really need to. Santa came to our house every year and he would come this year. Why would he not? The school Christmas play at the end of the week meant Christmas itself was only a few days away. All of our parents would come to the school for the program. We scrambled to be ready.

How easy it was to distract us. How willing I was to be distracted.

At the end of the day, we crowded into the unheated entryway of the school, pulled on our boots, tied flannel scarves around our heads, struggled into our heavy winter coats. As we spilled out into the schoolyard, we saw that the snow falling all day had almost erased the tracks of our recess Fox and Goose game. The snowmen we'd built a couple of days before and that had begun to melt in yesterday's sun now wore two inches of snow balanced in steep ridges on their tree twig arms. The snow was so deep that we didn't even need to use the stile to get across the fence. We could step right across the top wire on the crusted drifts.

Traipsing through the field toward home, we skittered light as dry leaves across the top of some drifts, broke through from time to time into snow up to our knees, waded out, flopped down to make snow angels, felt the snow melt in our boots. Alternately, we tilted our faces toward the sky to catch snowflakes on our tongues and tucked our heads down against gusts of wind. Plowing ahead into the biting east wind, we were soon coated with snow and could have been mistaken for the snowmen we left back in the schoolyard.

By the time we made it to the house, Larry's challenge had slid further into the back of my mind. When we opened the back door, my concerns about Santa were erased by the aroma of fresh-baked bread. As we struggled back out of our coats and boots, Mom called, "Who wants a slice of fresh bread?"

"I do, I do!" we shouted. We turned our boots upside down on newspapers that lined the back porch to let the melting snow trickle out and propped our wet mittens to dry against the kitchen heat registers.

The six big loaves of bread Mom baked that afternoon were lined up on the counter and the aroma of fresh bread filled the house. We crowded around the cutting board as Mom sliced off both hot heels from a loaf. Just like always, I claimed one heel and Sue grabbed the other. Settled around the table, we spread on thick layers of butter and bit into the warm, crusty bread.

Mom poured herself a cup of coffee and sat down with us. "Now tell me what went on at school today," she asked. "Did you have a chance to recite the poem Grandma Denter taught you?"

"Yes, we did," we chirped. "We said it all the way through, and everybody laughed. Want to hear it again?" I asked. "C'mon," I said, signaling to Jane and Sue. Without waiting, we slipped off our chairs, stood straight as toy soldiers, hands by our sides, and began in unison:

> "One day Mr. Santa Claus said to his wife,
> I'm tired of reindeer, I am on my life.
> You see we are living in an up-to-date age
> Where airships and motors are now quite the rage.
> And I'm really beginning to feel
> That I must buy me an automobile ..."

Grandma Denter had brought the poem with her when she came to visit us that fall, arriving as she usually did, a few weeks after Grandma Jensen went back to live with Aunt Joyce's family. One time—only once—both grandmas came to visit at the same time. When I asked Mom why they didn't visit together again, all Mom said was, "Too many cooks."

My grandmas were about as opposite as night and day. Grandma Jensen was tall and thin and as practical as a heavy sweatshirt in a chilly winter house, more prone to frown than smile. Grandma Denter was about as big around as she was tall and a smile never left her face. She loved to dress up in fancy hats and jewelry. And she loved to tell jokes.

When she arrived, we trailed her into the bedroom and crawled up on the bed while she unpacked her suitcase. Winking at me, she'd said, "Did I ever tell you girls about …"

"Tell us, tell us," we'd urged at once.

"All right then," she'd say as she settled into a chair and smoothed her apron over her lap. And she'd launch into a story.

When she finished telling the story, Grandma would clasp her hands across her stomach and lean back in the chair, a satisfied grin on her face. We clapped our hands and laughed, encouraging her to tell us story after story. Grandma entertained us with jokes and stories every day that she visited. When she wasn't telling us stories, she was having us memorize things, like the Lord's Prayer in German.

So it was no surprise to us when she pulled the "Santa Claus" poem out of her suitcase. She wanted us to memorize it and shortly she decided we should recite the poem in the school Christmas program.

"Oh, Mother Denter," Mom said. "I'm sure Harriet has plans for what the girls should be doing."

Grandma Denter was not intimidated by anything, certainly not our teacher, and she was used to getting things she wanted so when Mom questioned taking the idea of the poem to Miss Fowler, she just folded her arms across her ample stomach, nodded and said, "Don't you worry. It will be fine." And it was.

From the moment Miss Fowler agreed, teaching us the poem became the focus of Grandma's time with us.

"Let's get in the spirit," she said each afternoon after we got home from school. She set the stage for practice by preparing a big batch of egg nog, cracking a half dozen fresh eggs in a bowl and whipping them until the bubbly yellow foam was thick around the edges. We watched as she beat in milk, sugar and vanilla, and poured the thick, creamy egg nog into tall glasses. Topping the foam with a rich sprinkle of nutmeg, she handed a glass to each of us. Between sips, she coached us verse after verse until we all three had the poem memorized.

When Grandma finally went back to Wisconsin at the end of her visit, we were sorry to see her go. That was good egg nog. And the poem was planted so deep in our brains that Jane could recite it 50 years later.

"That was perfect, girls," Mom applauded when we finished reciting the poem and bowed low. "Grandma would be so proud of you."

The crumbs of our after-school snack brushed away, we checked out the growing piles of gifts under the silver Christmas tree in the living room. Every day we came home to find more packages, each one neatly labeled with one of our names.

Between new snow and fresh bread and barn chores and checking out my presents, the challenge to Santa's existence never returned to my mind.

This is how Christmas went at our house. On Christmas Eve, all the normal tasks were tinged with urgency and anticipation. We hurried to milk cows, hurried through supper, hurried to get dressed and to church. And all the while, my stomach was doing little flip-flops as I thought about presents and Santa. I loved everything about Christmas Eve.

In the dark, in a cold so crisp our boots crunched loud in the snow and our breath hung in crystal clouds on the air, we trooped into the warmth of the church. Inside, all the white light bulbs lining the sanctuary were replaced with blue bulbs, bulbs that created a cool aura of magic that befit a magic night. A huge evergreen tree cut from a farm field and draped with the construction paper chains we made in Sunday School class filled so much of the front of the church that the organ had to be moved to one side to make room.

The pews of our little country church were filled to capacity. Sitting hip by hip with my family for warmth and so there was enough room for everyone, we sang carols and listened as the minister read the Christmas story from the Gospel of Luke. As he read, my lips moved as I whispered the words; I could repeat the story from memory.

After the service was over, after they turned out the blue lights and we lit candles and sang Silent Night, one of the men passed out boxes of rock candy to each child. Then we piled back into our car for a ride home that was so short the car barely got warm. The rest of the evening we opened presents and prepared for Santa.

We all got presents for each other; gifts that accumulated under the Christmas tree for days before Christmas. Sometimes we made these presents. We could count on a bowl of cookies for each of us from Mom, for instance. One year I made place mats for Mom, using white Huck toweling and pink thread to make Christmas tree designs. For weeks I hunkered down behind the sofa, out of sight, to make these place mats and keep them a surprise.

Dad was the tough one to find a gift for. One year

I asked him what he wanted for Christmas. He thought for a minute and said, "A bull chain or a heat houser." I didn't know what a heat houser was so I looked into getting a bull chain, which is a very heavy, very strong chain Dad hooked to the ring in the bull's nose to lead him around when he took him out of the stall. The chain cost more money than I had to spend so I wound up getting him a bag of chocolate-covered peanuts. He said he liked that just as well.

That Christmas Eve, when we were barely back in the door from church, the phone rang and I leapt to answer it.

"Santa Claus is HERE! He's passing out presents right NOW!!!" Jeannie screamed through the receiver. "Look out your window; I bet you can see the reindeer and sleigh."

I slammed down the phone, not even taking time to say good bye. "Santa Claus is across the road," I shouted and Jane and Sue and I ran to the bedrooms on the north side of our house. All the north windows faced the highway with a clear view to Scheckels' house. We crowded against the window in our bedroom, scanning the clear night sky.

"Get out of the way, I want to see," I said, elbowing Sue away.

"Stop it or I'll tell," Sue elbowed back. "I want to see, too."

"I wonder if he'll come here next?" Sue asked, breathless.

"He has to," I responded. "It only makes sense. Why would he go anywhere else before coming here?"

We strained our necks and our eyes watching the dark sky. We did not even blink. When a half-hour had passed and we'd seen nary a reindeer, Jane called Jeannie back.

"We've been watching ever since you called," she said. "We didn't see anything."

And Santa was already gone.

This was a puzzle. Santa never came to our house on Christmas Eve. Santa always came to our house early on Christmas morning, before we got up. It had never happened any other way. But there we were, with proof that Santa had been right across the highway, right at that very minute. We had to be able to see him. He had to come to our house next. And yet he didn't come to our house. And we didn't see him.

We pulled ourselves away from the windows.

"I'm sure you just looked away at the moment he flew away," Mom said, herding us back into the living room.

"I can't believe we missed him. How could he get away so fast?" I slumped on the couch.

"Santa can do just about anything he wants to," Mom responded with irrefutable logic.

"But why wouldn't he come here next if he was right across the road?" I persisted.

"I'm sure he has a system worked out. Don't worry, I'm sure he'll get back here sometime tonight. Now let's open our presents," Mom turned to the tree. "And you have to get your stockings ready before it's bed time."

I thought about Larry's comments at school, but I did not bring it up. I just couldn't.

It didn't take long to open presents even though we did it systematically. Only one person opened a gift at a time and everyone watched them do it, unless we were pretty sure we were all getting the same thing. Like a bowl of chocolate oatmeal cookies.

Before we went to bed, we arranged everything to

be ready for Santa to come. We each had a big red flannel stocking with our name written on it in black magic marker. We dragged the kitchen chairs into the living room and hung our stockings from knobs on the backs of these chairs. We made sure there was plenty of room around each chair and that our name on the stocking was in plain sight so Santa would not be confused.

We fixed a plate of sugar cookies topped with red and green sugar crystals (Santa's favorite, Mom assured us) and a glass of milk and left these beside a stack of carrots on the kitchen table. We also left a note: "Dear Santa: These cookies and the milk are for you. The carrots are for the reindeer. Thank you for all the presents. Love, Jane, Carol, Sue."

"You better get to bed now," Mom urged. "Santa won't come if you don't."

We kissed Dad good night and Mom tucked us into bed. Jane had her own room. Sue and I slept together in another bedroom.

"When do you think Santa will come?" I whispered to Sue.

"I don't know, but I'm going to stay awake." We said this every year.

"Do you think he'll be able to get down the chimney?" I asked. We went to the basement every year to talk through the logistics of this feat. There was just no denying that we had a very skinny chimney with an even smaller clean-out door. We agreed that the chimney was too small for anyone to get down, let alone someone with Santa's girth, and even if someone came down, they'd land in the wood-burning furnace and burn up. If he came down the chimney, it had to be magic.

"He must come in the doors," I reasoned.

"How does he get down off the roof where the reindeer land?" Sue asked. We knew for a fact he landed the sleigh on the roof because one year it snowed on Christmas Eve and on Christmas Day Dad showed us Santa's footprints in the snow on the roof.

We continued to talk through Santa logistics until Dad growled, "Quiet down in there," from the living room where he and Mom were watching the news before they went to bed. We giggled.

"Santa won't come if you're still awake." Mom's more gentle voice drifted in on the heels of Dad's growl.

Pulling the blankets up over our heads, we agreed to be quiet for two minutes. In two minutes it was morning. Almost morning. It was dark when Sue poked me in the shoulder.

"I'm going to go see if Santa has been here," she whispered and slipped out of bed. Within seconds of creeping down the hall to the living room she came tearing back and jumped on the bed. "He's been here, he's been here! Get up. Let's open presents."

In a flash we were both up and we went to get Jane. We tore back down the hall, past Mom and Dad's room. We didn't know how early it must really have been. Dad was always up at 4 a.m. to start the milking chores yet he was still in bed.

I crept in and tapped Dad's shoulder, "Santa's been here. We're going to open presents," I whispered.

Dad groaned, rolled over, woke Mom and they followed us into the living room. Mom plugged in the lights on the tree and we opened presents in the glow of red, green, yellow and blue bubble-light candles. One white light glowed from the tin foil covered cardboard star at the very top.

I headed straight for the chair where my big red stocking bulged with little toys, candy and an orange. I would also check way down in the toe of the stocking, something we all did ever since the year we almost missed finding rings in the very toe tips. This year, however, I bypassed all that and sank right to the floor in happy bliss.

There was Trigger, just as I saw him in the Christmas catalog, just as he existed in my dreams. Roy Rogers was in the saddle holding the reins in one hand while he waved his other hand. Santa Claus came through again.

On New Year's Eve—the one night of the year we were allowed to stay up until midnight—Zidlickys came to our house to visit. Our parents played cards. Meanwhile, their kids—Jolynn and Paul—joined us roaming from basement to attic. In the course of the evening, we feasted on oyster stew and Norwegian foods like lutefisk and lefse. Sharing our new toys from Christmas was the highlight.

"Look what Santa brought me," I gloated as I showed Paul my Roy Rogers and Trigger.

"There isn't any Santa," Paul stated, the sound of his voice blunt and hard on my ears.

Staring back at Paul's pale blue eyes, I wanted nothing more than to slap his fat face. "Is too," I said, but tears sprang up in my eyes and I turned my back to Paul so he wouldn't see.

Something in the way he said it, something in my mind that couldn't reconcile Santa at a neighbor's on Christmas Eve but not at our house until Christmas morning, something in the mounting number of kids who kept saying Santa wasn't real, sent me to Mom a few days later.

"Mom, Paul says there's no Santa," I said, my lower lip quivering, as I looked up at her standing by the stove. "There is, isn't there?"

She looked at me and hesitated. "Let's go in the bedroom," she said at last, wiping her hands on her apron.

Mom led me into her bedroom, closed the door, and came to sit beside me on the bed. The morning sun glared off the snow and through the window, illuminating dust particles that floated in the air and landed on the maple dresser. Mom was quiet, too quiet, I thought, when she said, "Honey, Santa is very important to all of us."

"But he is real, right?" I pushed. I looked up at her, maybe already knowing the answer, but I had to make her say it anyway.

"Honey, Santa teaches us about getting presents and giving them."

I listened as Mom talked. She never answered my question. In that moment, I felt old and silly. I wanted Santa to be real and the tears streamed down my cheeks.

"What about the Easter Bunny?" I asked. I did not hear what she said. I expect I didn't need to. No one past the age of four could really believe rabbits deliver eggs. I enjoyed Easter morning with the basket and hunting for chocolate eggs, but this one I supposed I could shrug off.

"The tooth fairy?" I asked at last, swallowing the hard reality even before she confirmed the suspicion. When she nodded again, I sat there, shoulders hunched, tears wet on my cheeks. Mom kept her arm tight around my shoulders and didn't say anything else.

I thought about Santa Claus, the Easter Bunny, the Tooth Fairy. I thought about the last tooth Dad pulled for me. He and I were the only ones to know about that. No one else knew when I snuck that tooth under my pillow. It was a secret . . .

Then I realized that Dad was in on this, too, and I felt even sillier. Of course, Dad would talk to Mom. It was, however, the first time I realized Mom and Dad were in cahoots, that the secrets I thought I had just with Dad maybe weren't.

"Carol," Mom broke into my painful reverie, "it's important for children to believe in Santa. You enjoyed this for a long time. Now you are old enough to help little ones like Sue have dreams."

Just like that I jumped across a chasm from one world into another. It was all as brilliantly and painfully clear as the morning sun reflecting off the fresh January snow. I squinted against the sun and rocked back and forth in this new, unwelcome knowledge. At that moment, Larry pushed his way back into my mind. I could see plain as day all of us kids standing around our teacher's desk. I remembered how I'd felt having Miss Fowler support me about Santa, and how angry and confused and maybe even hurt Larry had looked. And here he was right and I was wrong. I didn't know what I'd say to him now.

Mom gave me a hug, kissed me on the forehead, and left the bedroom, closing the door behind her. I sat on the edge of the bed and then tipped over, curling into a tight ball, giving myself over to crying for dreams I could never get back.

In live theater, they call it "the willing suspension of disbelief," the ability of the audience to accept that for the duration of the play, what happens up on the stage is real. Looking back, I am mildly embarrassed to admit that I willingly suspended disbelief for nearly 12 years, an unbelievably long time for a child to believe in the Triple Crown of childhood fantasies.

It speaks to the times, though, and the place. The middle of the 20th century, a farm in rural Iowa. A time and a place where a child could just go on believing.

Making Hay

The sun was a glare, the July air dripping with humidity so heavy even the flies thought twice about moving off the window screens when Dad and the hired men came in from the field and retreated to the cool dark of the basement to wash up before dinner. I finished setting the table and followed the men downstairs. Sure enough, Dad had opened the basement fridge and pulled out cold bottles of Schlitz. The bottles sweated cold beads of moisture in the hands of the men who were still sweating themselves. As each one took turns washing up at the small sink, scrubbing sweat and hay dust off with the coarse bar of Lava, the others sat, welcoming the break from the blazing sun of the open fields.

I sidled up to Dad. "Can I have a sip?" I whispered.

"She can hear a bottle of beer open from the Back 40," he laughed, and I felt a ripple of pleasure as he looked at the men and handed me his bottle.

I tipped a little of the bitter gold liquid into my mouth and handed the bottle back to him. One sip was all I wanted. One sip brought me into the circle of the men.

If I couldn't actually work with the men, I could soak in their talk. I could pretend. I could dream. I leaned against Dad's leg, listening as the men talked about haying—how many loads they'd put up this morning, how far they figured they'd get in the afternoon.

When it was time to make hay, Dad headed to the field with the hired men as soon as the dew dried. As long as the weather was good, they didn't leave the fields except to come in for dinner. The men radiated the aura of strength and power in their work. I hung around them soaking in that strength though I was, according to Dad, too young and 'too light in the poop' to do more than help Mom with meals.

While the men made hay, the kitchen filled with the sounds of ladles banged against pans and silverware clattering as Mom prepared the noon meal. Each night, Mom selected a roast for the next day's meal from the freezer and set it out to thaw. After we downed a breakfast that included fried eggs, bacon and fried potatoes, she browned the roast and put it in the Dutch oven to cook slowly. By noon, the roast was so tender you didn't need a knife to cut it.

In the course of the morning, she'd eventually say to one of us kids, "Go pull some onions and radishes."

"How many? How big?" we'd ask as we headed out to the garden.

"Oh, about that many and about that big," she'd respond. "Enough for everyone to eat," she added, shooing us out the door. We'd go get them and somehow whatever we carried in would be just right. Occasionally Mom joined us to pick peas or green beans. We worked our way down the row, turning the vines from side to side, testing the pods with a gentle squeeze, holding the vines so the roots stayed secure in the ground as we pulled mature pods free. Pods quickly mounded in the pan Mom nudged down the row with her toe.

I liked to pick peas, or more accurately, I liked to eat peas. For each pod I picked, I'd find another one to eat. "Look at this one. It has nine peas," I'd exclaim after I slit open a pod and just before I tilted it above my mouth, letting the perfect, sweet peas dribble onto my tongue.

Back in the house, Mom directed, "Go get a dozen potatoes." She was always in motion and we were additional arms and legs. I took a pan down to the fruit cellar in the basement, pulling the string that hung by the door to turn on the bare light bulb.

The cool, musty, earthy smell of the fruit cellar was comforting and reassuring. If we were attacked by the Russians or they dropped a nuclear bomb on us, I thought this would be a good place to wait until the radiation was gone.

The news was full of reports advising everyone to have an air raid shelter and a plan for being safe in case the Russians attacked. Mom and Dad talked about it, too, and I listened with a mixture of anxiety and excitement. We had a cement cistern and I'd never been down in it, but Sue and I did sometimes lift the heavy metal lid to look inside. It was dark but we could see some water and some trash. It definitely didn't seem like a good place to have to spend any time.

I debated with Jane whether we would get bombed or not. "I don't think so," I said one day. "Why would they bomb us? If they were going to attack the United States, they'd want the food we produce. Wouldn't they?" I asked, hoping against anxiety this would be true.

"Yes, but we're close to Chicago," Jane worried.

"They'd attack where there were a lot of people. And the missile silos are by Omaha. They'd have to bomb those."

During those times, I watched the night sky to the north, half expecting to see Russian fighters screaming toward us. Russian soldiers haunted my dreams and I plotted all kinds of places to hide. In the house, I considered the attic crawl space under the eaves as a possibility but discarded this as a real option because there was only one way in or out and no room to run. The bins in the corncrib also received consideration. Running along at such a height, balanced only on the two-by-four boards that separated one bin from another, intimidated me, so I did not count this a prime hiding place either. I felt most at ease when I thought of the gullies in open fields and the trees in the Back 40. The Russians would not know the route I'd taken and I could keep moving anywhere, all the time. Thoughts of avoiding the Russians consumed a major portion of my brain for quite some time.

Dad wasn't inclined to build a special shelter so as a family we eventually decided on the basement fruit cellar as the place we would go should a bomb drop. The basement was also our retreat from tornadoes: the southwest corner of the basement, under a table.

I did worry that the small window in the fruit cellar would let in nuclear rays that would no doubt bounce off the walls like a cue ball careening around a pool table, but I figured we were mainly underground so maybe the radiation couldn't get us. At least we'd have food. We could stay there for a long time.

The walls of the fruit cellar were lined with shelves. Each shelf was a constantly shifting storehouse of two-quart jars, quart jars and pints of fruits and vegetables, jams and pickles. No sooner had we canned vegetables that ripened in the garden and placed them on these shelves, than we retrieved jars for the next meal. Toward the end of the winter there may be fewer full jars, but the shelves were never empty.

Now that it was summer, the metal trough at the end of the fruit cellar that we had filled with potatoes last year was close to empty, and I had to search for firm potatoes. That spring, we'd taken out potatoes that had started to grow sprouts, cut them into sections and planted hills in long rows in the garden. As early as June, when the potatoes we'd planted were nowhere near mature, we sometimes dug a hill or two anyway, searching for the tiny new potatoes. These tiny/walnut/baby-sized potatoes were so tender Mom didn't even have to peel them before she cooked a summer favorite—creamed new potatoes and peas. Later in the summer, when the potato vines shriveled and dried, the potatoes we carried from the garden in bushel baskets filled the bin again. Seldom did we run out.

When I brought up the potatoes, Mom set Grandma up to peel them. Grandma Jensen sat by the table, the pan of potatoes wedged between her knees, her print housedress drawn up revealing rolled-down nylons. Grandma was skilled with a paring knife, sometimes managing to peel an entire potato so the peel held in one long spiral. She cut each potato in quarters and dropped the pieces in the pan of cold water Mom set next to her on the table.

"Can I have a piece?" I asked Grandma.

"You'll spoil your dinner," she said, turning a stern look on me.

"Oh, come on. Just one?"

"Just one won't hurt, Mother," Mom said.

"Go ahead then," Grandma said with a grunt.

It was as though Grandma believed the end of the

world would come if we ate a potato, I thought. I took a slice, tapped the water off against the side of the pan, sprinkled it with salt and bit into the crisp, white spear.

Mom smiled at me as she slid two pies into the oven. She'd rolled out crusts and made pies for dinner and supper that day. The bubbling pies would come out of the oven by 11:30 so they'd cool enough to serve for dessert but still be warm. I do not ever recall a piece left over.

All this, or something very like it, was going on upstairs that July as I stood by my dad's knee listening to the men talk about making hay. Their conversation came to a halt when Mom shouted down the stairs.

"Come and get it before I throw it to the dogs."

Dad drained the last drops of beer, handed the empty Schlitz bottle to me to put in the case and stood up. "Let's go. Ma won't wait."

At exactly noon the men sat down at the table. Dinner was always on the table at exactly noon. Dad could work all morning and count on coming in from the fields and finding it ready. Mom could fix the meal, timing every bowl to hit the table at noon, and count on the men being there to eat it. Roast beef, potatoes, gravy, homemade bread, creamed peas, pickles, apple pie.

Once we'd all sat down, Mom turned to Jane. "Would you say the prayer, please?" Table grace signaled the start of every meal and was followed by a stream of serving dishes passed to the left.

"Dry!" Sue blurted so loudly and suddenly that the hired men looked up from their plates in surprise. Sue's shout signaled the start of a three-second game we kids played at every meal.

The game related to washing dishes at the end of

a meal. It worked like this. We divided dishes into three tasks: washing (least desirable), drying (most desirable), and rinsing/putting dishes away (acceptable). The rule was that none of us could lay claim to a task before the meal started. The first person to think of it after the meal started shouted out their preferred task—almost always drying. Then it was a question of whose reflexes were fast enough to avoid having to wash.

"Rinse and put away," I sputtered through a full mouth.

"Oh, nuts," Jane muttered. She would stand at the sink again. Over the years, Jane lost so frequently I came to harbor the suspicion she actually liked to wash.

"Be quiet now," Dad said as he turned on the radio to catch the noon market reports. Immediately all talk stopped while the announcer read the day's prices for hogs, cattle and corn. Anyone who talked after the announcer started reeling off the day's prices earned a knuckle thunk on the head. Dad turned off the radio as soon as the farm report was finished and conversation rose around the table as though it had been switched on when the radio was switched off.

"We'll get going in a half-hour," Dad said, after the pie was gone and a last cup of coffee drained. Chairs scuffed back from the table as the men rose and went outside to let dinner settle. Lighting cigarettes, or lying on the ground under the walnut tree by the pump stand, arms flung over their eyes to block the light, they rested. While they lay down outside, Dad took his nap on the kitchen floor, a small pillow under his head.

"Wake me up in 15 minutes," he said to Mom. Even on a hard floor in the middle of the kitchen, Dad was snoring in under a minute. We tiptoed around and over him, clearing the table, washing the dishes, and cleaning up from dinner.

Mom woke Dad up in exactly 15 minutes. Once she'd thought he could use a little extra rest and let him sleep a half-hour. When she did wake him and he realized he'd lost that time, he grumbled a harsh, "Damn it, Ma," that made my skin curl. Probably hers, too. After that, she woke him exactly when he asked.

Getting up as though he hadn't just been snoring loud enough to wake the dead, Dad pulled on his work shoes, grabbed his hat from the hook by the back door and headed out. "Let's go, men," he called and the men sleeping or smoking under the walnut tree pulled to their feet and made for the tractor and hayrack.

While haying was going on, in addition to having a full breakfast on the table at 7 a.m., a full dinner on the table at exactly noon, and a full supper on the table at 7 p.m., Mom fixed lunch and took it to the field in the mid-afternoon.

"Grab the thermos bottles." Mom motioned toward the counter. "We can meet the tractor at the top of the hill." Mom stacked the ice water chocolate cake she made that afternoon on top of a Tupperware container of lunch meat and cheese sandwiches and headed for the door. With a big silver thermos of coffee in one hand and a two-quart jar of ice water in the other, I backed through the door, bracing it open with my back so Mom could edge through.

Once we had everything in the pickup, Mom wrestled the old Studebaker out across the field while I held the coffee and water jugs upright on the floor between my feet and kept a hand on the sandwiches and cake so they didn't bounce off the seat. We careened over ruts, stirring up a cloud of dust behind us.

Mom stopped the truck on a hill a ways in front of the oncoming baler. As soon as I swung open the door and stepped out onto the hay stubble, I realized I should have put on shoes before I left the house. Stepping on hay stubble feels every bit like stepping on the point ends of spikes. I stepped lightly, planted my feet in between the hay stubble when I could and pretended it didn't hurt when I couldn't. We left lunch on the truck seat and leaned against the fender, watching the tractor and hayrack crawl toward us.

I shaded my eyes, squinting into the sun, to see the men work. Their muscles rippled and sweat streamed down their faces and arms. They wore leather gloves but the young men often stripped off their shirts and their bodies glistened strong and hard in the afternoon sun. They were doing important work and when we brought lunch to the field, I felt I was doing something important, too.

One of the men drove the tractor and another walked alongside, picking up bales and throwing them up onto the hayrack. Dad grabbed hold of the twine binding each 70-pound bale and fitted the bales tight onto the stack. Each bale had to be in the right place so the load held together as the wagon rocked back and forth over the rolling hills. Finishing the field would have gone faster except one of the men had left at noon.

As they slowed to a stop, Mom began pulling the food out of the truck. The men climbed down, wiping sweat from their heads and necks. I was ready with the water they always wanted first. Dad took the jar from my hands and drank in big gulps.

"Thanks, Squirt," he said. "That hit the spot." He handed the jar on to the hired men, picked up a sandwich and sat down on the ground in the shade of the tractor. The hired men lounged on the hayrack, grateful for the shade cast by the half load of sweet-smelling hay bales.

"We'll finish this field today and then we'll just have that piece over behind Millers for tomorrow," he said, nodding toward the southeast. "It's slow going since Tom left." He took off his cap and wiped the sweat off his head before settling his cap firmly back in place. "Hand me a piece of that cake, Squirt," he said.

I grabbed the cake pan and took it to Dad. If I put my feet down just right, I could slide my bare soles between most of the stubble. Still I must have looked comical as I tottered in a bowlegged roll between the truck, tractor and hayrack.

As Dad took a big piece of cake, he said, "Squirt, suppose you can drive the tractor for the rest of this round?"

My head jerked up and a thrill ran straight through my stomach. Jane had driven the tractor already, but Dad had never let me.

"Sure," I said, and it was all I could do to keep from hopping up onto the tractor seat right that minute. It took a moment for me to remember that I didn't know how to drive the tractor but I wasn't going to say anything about that little detail.

When the last bit of cake was gone followed by a last swallow of coffee, the men lumbered to their feet, thanked Mom for the lunch and stretched to loosen their sore backs. Then Dad looked at me and said, "Ready?"

I sure was. In a second, I'd stepped from the toolbar up to the torn, sweat-stained, padded tractor seat. With the wheel of the Farmall H firmly in my grasp, I realized I had only the vaguest notion what to do next. Dad had held me on his lap while he'd driven the tractors, but I'd never done more than put my tiny hands on the wheel next to his. My stomach flipped. Would Dad make me get down?

If Dad sensed my hesitation, he didn't let on. He stood on the toolbar, his left arm on the back of the seat. "See if it's in neutral," he said wiggling the stick shift between my knees. "The brake is set, so step on the clutch. Push it all the way in," he directed. I grabbed hold of the wheel with both hands and put my whole 70 pounds into pushing the clutch all the way forward. My butt rose up off the seat as I pulled back on the wheel to get enough leverage to push the pedal down. Sweat broke out on my neck. I was unsure how long I could hold the pedal down.

"Now push the starter," Dad said. I didn't know that letting go of the wheel long enough to push the starter was such a hot idea, but I couldn't say so. I let go with my right hand and reached down, pressing the starter with my thumb. The tractor sputtered to life and I could feel the engine strain against my arms and legs like a cow pulling against a halter.

"We'll put it in first," he said, maneuvering the stick into gear. "Now, let the pedal out easy. Don't jerk it or you'll kill it."

I eased back on the pedal. The tractor jerked. I killed it. I was mortified.

Grabbing the steering wheel so tight my fingers hurt, I strained to push the clutch pedal down again. With Dad's hand over mine, I moved the stick into neutral and pushed the starter again. The old tractor coughed to life and Dad shifted into first.

"We'll give it a little gas," Dad said as he pulled the throttle a couple notches toward me. "Now let the pedal out."

The tractor lurched but kept running. "Now just keep her going straight."

"But what about stopping," I asked, thinking already that stopping on my own was going to be tougher than starting with Dad by my side.

"When we get to the end of the row, step on the clutch and brake pedals at the same time," Dad said as he stepped from the toolbar onto the tongue of the wagon and back to the hayrack.

Anxious, I looked ahead. With relief I saw the end of the row was a long ways away.

I could not believe it. I looked at Mom standing by the truck. She smiled and waved. I looked back at Dad balancing on the hayrack. "Give it a little more gas," he yelled. I reached forward and eased the throttle lever toward me two more notches. I looked back again. Dad was grabbing bales from two men now and the load was filling fast. He was not at all concerned about me.

A moment like this, experiencing such power, I wondered if I looked as different as I felt.

The steering wheel fought against me with each bump we hit and my hands ached from holding on tight. I did not care. Dad entrusted me with this great responsibility. Struggling to keep the tractor headed perfectly straight, I moved from the world of dreaming, of pretending, to the real world. Just like that, I was working with the men.

Ashes

In all the years I was growing up, I can count on three fingers the times we took a vacation that didn't involve going to stay with relatives. One of those was the trip to Stone City, a trip burned into my memory not so much for itself as for our return home and the losses that followed.

The day of the trip, the alarm jangled and I awoke, my pajamas tangled around my arms and legs. I'd kicked the sheets off the end of the bed in the night in a fitful effort to find a cool place for my feet. Faint breaths of warm air carrying the sweet scent of new-mown hay drifted through the screen of the bedroom window. Rubbing sleepers out of my eyes, I got up, pulled on my shorts and buttoned up a sleeveless shirt as I slid my feet into the rubber thongs that had become my favorite footwear. They had the great advantage of going from dirty to clean under the faucet outside the back door. Mom bought them for me to wear to swimming lessons, but I now wore them anytime I couldn't go barefoot. Except to church.

Sue rolled out of bed right behind me. After we'd pulled up the sheets and spread, smoothing them over the pillows, we headed out to do the barn chores. The morning sun glared red on the horizon, promising another hot July day. As we shuffled down the hill toward the barn, dew on the grass was chilly wet on my toes. "No rain today," I observed. Dad always said if there was dew, it meant no rain; if there was no dew, it very likely would rain.

Dad watched the weather signs every day, particularly when he had hay to put up. "Got that last cutting in without a drop of rain on it," he'd comment in an off-handed way to a neighbor, as though it didn't mean particularly much. "Yup. That'll be good hay," the neighbor would respond.

In an unspoken competition, Dad and the other farmers watched each other, noting who got crops in first, whose hay was cut but still in the field when it rained, who kept weeds mowed in pastures and who didn't, who still had corn standing in the field when it snowed. Observations such as these were shared every night when we had supper and it wasn't long before we kids were keeping an eye on our neighbors, too. The neighborhood was tight-knit. Through an unbroken grapevine of casual conversation at the feed store, at the gas station, after church let out, or by phone when it was urgent, they also knew who needed help. Then they offered that help quietly or they just showed up.

Dad and the hired men had finished putting up the second cutting of hay earlier in the week, the bales stacked high in the new barn south of the milking parlor. That meant there wouldn't be hired men at dinner and so we'd be able to take the drive Mom had promised again last night.

"I want you girls to see some things," she explained when we asked where we were going and why. "It will be a little vacation," she added. Her words sent a thrill of anticipation rippling up my spine. A trip that had no useful purpose like getting groceries or a part for the tractor. A day devoted to just driving somewhere unknown. A few hours when who knows what might happen. I was ready.

Mom said that Grant Wood, a famous artist, had lived in Stone City. I fancied myself to have a future as an artist. After I finished my assignments at school, I went to the bookshelf and pulled down the "H" encyclopedia. It held pages of pictures of all different kinds of horses. Arabians. Quarter Horses. Palominos. And my favorite, Indian Ponies. Little Joe Cartwright rode an Indian pony on *Bonanza*. Horses were far and away my favorite thing to draw, and I drew them all the time.

I saw the ads in Dad's Successful Farming magazine, the ads claiming I might have a real future as an artist. If I just drew the Pirate and sent it in, Real Professionals would assess my talent. I could not imagine quite how it worked, but I believed if I could re-create that exact Pirate, exactly as he appeared in the drawing, I would win. I would be judged a Talented Artist. In my bedroom, door closed from the prying eyes of my sisters, I drew the Pirate, spirited a stamp and envelope from Dad's desk drawer in the kitchen, and ran my drawings to the mailbox. My sisters and Mom and Dad would be so surprised when I won.

I ignored the tiny detail that I had drawn the pirate and the cowboy in a similar ad and sent them in several times before and heard nothing. I figured the Real Professionals were busy with their own art, or I hadn't made my copy exact enough, or my letter got lost, or their letter to me got lost. Nowhere in my thinking did it occur to me they thought I had no talent. Of course I had talent. My teacher Miss Fowler said so and so did Mom when I showed her the horses I drew.

One year I positioned a card table by my bedroom window intent on sketching the hills, trees and fields north of our house. I imagined myself painting stunning landscapes with my eight-color watercolor set and the leftover paints from my last paint-by-number project. The results were more akin to cave drawings. Nothing I drew looked remotely like anything I saw in the magazines Mom stacked away in the crawl space of the attic. I abandoned my studio after a few days, discouraged. Then in a little while the idea would flit through my mind again, like a migrating bird in the spring, and I'd pull out pencils and paints and crayons to try once more.

But now, NOW, I was going to get to see where a real artist painted. By seeing where he worked, by seeing what he saw when he painted, I could figure out how to paint like a real artist.

On the day of our trip to Stone City, Mom finished packing a lunch and Grandma Jensen put away the last of the breakfast dishes as we girls changed into clean shorts and shirts. The sun was up full in the sky, the heat undeterred by the least wisp of cloud. Sweat beads collected under my bangs, trickling between my shoulder blades as we piled into our black Chevrolet sedan. Jane sat in front between Mom and Grandma because she always got carsick, leaving the back seat to Sue and me.

Earlier that morning, Dad filled the car up from the barrel of gas he used to fill the tractors. Gas was 24 cents a gallon in town; it was cheaper bought in bulk. Plus, Mom wouldn't have to stop for gas on the trip.

"We'll be back in time for milking," Mom said to Dad as she stowed a picnic lunch in the trunk, climbed into the front seat and turned the ignition. Sue and I knelt on the back seat, waving out the window at Dad who disappeared in the cloud of dust stirred up as we motored up the lane.

Mom drove often enough—to town for groceries,

to 4-H meetings on neighboring farms, to Sunday school activities. But driving was, for the most part, Dad's job, a man's job. Some of the neighbor women didn't drive at all. When Mom got behind the steering wheel, she gripped the wheel with both hands and never let go. Her back was ramrod straight and she leaned slightly forward to better see the road and anything that might be on it. She held this at-attention position until we arrived at our destination, whether 15 minutes or two hours later, all the while chewing vigorously on a stick of gum.

As Mom negotiated the two-lane highway and rolling hills of eastern Iowa, we entertained ourselves with car games, most of which depended on one of us being the first to spot something. We competed to be the first to see Burma Shave signs—words of wisdom on boards nailed to successive fence posts. We read in unison. "Big mistake ... Many make ... Rely on horn ... Instead of brake ... Burma Shave." Each completed sequence resulted in giggles and groans and a frantic effort to write down the words to tell Dad when we got back home.

We also kept a list of cars from other counties. Grandma had a prodigious memory for lists and could recite all 99 Iowa counties by name and number. She knew that Adair County was Number 1 as well as she knew that Jackson County was 49, all the way up to Wright County at 99. So each time we spied a new number, the only county designation on license plates at that time, she told us the county name.

As we rolled over the last hills before the slow descent into the valley to Stone City, Sue and I pushed forward, craning to see everything as soon as humanly possible. Before long, our heads were fully in the front seat even though our bodies were technically still in the back. Bathed in the dusty golden sun, the valley was, I would come to learn, just as Grant Wood painted it—hilly corn and hay fields, trees in the fence rows—the ideal scene people visualize when they think of rural America.

When we finally arrived, I was vaguely disappointed in a way I couldn't quite define. Stone City was only a few buildings really, all made of big yellow limestone blocks from a local quarry. Billowing limestone dust followed us along the gravel roads and when Mom pulled into the churchyard at the top of a hill, yellow grit filtered out of the air and settled silent on the car. Dust already on the grass and the leaves of the huge, old oak trees surrounding the church made it seem as though we saw everything through a warm, amber filter. In the penetrating July sun, dust stuck to our sweaty bodies.

"Don't run in the church," Mom called, as we kids rushed inside while she and Grandma walked at a pace suited to the heat. Inside, the thick limestone walls provided cool darkness and a brief escape from the heat and glare of the sun. Golden light filtered through the tall, stained glass windows, creating a soft glow on the worn pews. We tiptoed down the aisle, dragging our fingers along the top of each pew. I gazed up at Christ on the cross. The light, the feel, it was a place I might have painted if I'd known how. It did not occur to me to wonder about Grant Wood.

In truth there was not much to see since Stone City was not a functioning town. There was an occupied house or two, no museum, no real store although there was a Coca-Cola machine into which we each slid a dime and pulled out a bottle of pop drenched at once in beads of moisture. While Mom and Grandma sat in the shade on a limestone bench, my sisters and I chased around under the trees, in and out of the buildings, threw sticks into the stream that ran through the valley. We were unimpressed by the few faded prints of Wood's paintings Mom discovered hanging on the dusty walls in the dark, cobwebby recesses of one of the buildings.

Within a short while, Mom got us all back into the car and we drove to Anamosa to the Grant Wood School, a one-room schoolhouse not at all dissimilar to our own. Nonetheless, we looked at everything, found desks that fit us, imagined for one second being painters because Mom suggested we should. How to become a painter was still a puzzle to me. The hills Grant Wood painted were our hills. His schoolhouse was like our school. His life—at least as much of it as I could see on this trip—seemed like my life.

As we tried one desk and then another, laughing at the strange familiarity of another country school—though one that turned out someone famous—how could we have known what was happening at home? We live our lives unaware of events happening around us that are destined to shape us.

By the time we came out of the school, Mom had unpacked our picnic lunch. We ate sitting on the dry grass in the shade of the car. All the car doors stood open to let the breeze—the only air conditioning we had available—blow through. The last syrupy sweet sips of my Coke bordered on being as hot as the sun reflecting off the car, but as I rolled the thick, green glass bottle between my hands I decided I liked it that way. I leaned back against the car, closed my eyes and breathed in the warm, dusty air, enjoying a day that was not so different from every day on the farm but that was, at the same time, very different.

In no time, Mom packed everything back up and we headed home. Sue and I lay down, head to head, our bare feet on opposite window frames, the wind whipping through the open windows warming and cooling us at the same time. We'd be home in time for milking at 5:00. Grandma could easily have supper on the table by 6:00.

Lying on the seat, my feet up against the window, I watched the sky cloud over and thought about the dew on the grass that morning. Maybe it would rain anyway; sometimes it did in spite of the signs. The closer we got to the farm, the heavier the clouds became until they were so thick and the sky so dark, it seemed like night.

"There sure are a lot of cars," Grandma observed when we were only a mile or so from the farm. Sue and I sat up as Grandma kept a running total of the cars we met.

"There are," Mom agreed. "I wonder if there's a fire somewhere?" she added idly.

Her comment set all of us to scanning the horizon for smoke. I recalled the recent fire on a neighbor's farm that burned the house down in the middle of the night. The family had kids our age and we'd listened in open-mouthed awe as they described escaping the house in the middle of the night wearing only their pajamas, scooting down the stairs on their butts because the stairs were too hot for their bare feet. They got out okay, but after that, everyone talked about keeping hard-soled shoes by your bed just in case.

The closer we got to our farm, the more cars there were. Grandma could barely keep up with her count. This many cars in late afternoon in rural Iowa was truly an uncommon thing. Mom gripped the steering wheel even more tightly in the face of this unexpected rural rush hour.

As we drew closer to our lane, we realized many of those cars were turning in, driving up the hill to our farm.

"Oh, no!" Mom exclaimed, her back and shoulders radiated anxiety as she edged forward into the steering wheel. Because it was so overcast, we had not seen smoke.

Nor had we seen flames. Still, my skin crawled with snakes of fear at the sound in Mom's voice. I wanted her to propel us immediately and directly home by her will, something I know she'd have done if she could.

We made it up the lane to see our yard full of cars. All our neighbors crowded the yard along with many people I didn't know.

Fire had destroyed the barn full of new-baled hay by the time we got there. The fire department arrived in time to keep the fire from spreading to any of the other buildings and now they were still spraying water, pulling down what was left of the charred roof and poles. For many hours neighbors drove tractors dragging chains through the smoldering hay to make sure the fire was out.

Spontaneous combustion, I heard the men say as I ran back and forth from the house to the barn with the sandwiches and thermos bottles of coffee Mom and Grandma made as fast and as easily as if they'd been planning all week to have several dozen visitors. Somehow in all that new hay, the men stacked a few bales that weren't completely dry. The moisture made heat as the hay dried. Heat trapped in the middle of the stack built up until it spontaneously started the dry hay bales on fire. All that work, the new hay barn, all up in smoke. Anxiety and excitement mixed up inside, giving me a painful stomach ache. Watching Dad, I could not see past the soot and rivulets of sweat running down his neck to how he felt.

The next day some neighbors returned and worked with Dad to clear away the rest of the burned-down building. There was nothing left of the hay to salvage.

That afternoon, when she was sure the fire was out, Mom brought us kids down to the barnyard. On any other day, we would have raced ahead, but now we clung to the safe haven of Mom's side. Almost afraid to look, we edged around her to stare at the remnants of charred beams and sodden hay bales. Mom stood shaking her head, her lips in a tight line, her hands resting on her hips, the hem of her cotton shirtwaist dress rippling in the breeze. As worry crinkled around in my stomach, I looked up at her. What did this mean to us? I didn't know.

After a bit, Mom reached down and picked up a piece of charcoal left by the fire. She stared at it for a few moments, then smiled at me, "Artists use charcoal like this to draw with. You could give it a try." I looked down at the charcoal and up at Mom. Then I knew it was all okay.

Over the course of the summer, Dad built another hay barn to replace the one that burned. And by the end of the summer, the new barn was filled with hay. What this cost or how he came up with the money or where the hay came from, I don't know. I do know there was no insurance. Dad and Mom didn't talk about things like this around us kids. They just managed.

I spent many days that summer trying my hand at charcoal drawing. It did not take long to learn that charcoal drawing, like other kinds of drawing and painting I'd tried, was not a talent of mine. Those failed artistic attempts left me with a sense of loss and a smoldering creative yearning that rekindled time and again over the years.

As a child I saw limited options. Art was drawings. Over time though, in part because of that summer, I came to realize that creativity takes many forms and charcoal can be used for writing as well as drawing.

My folks swept away the ashes and built a new barn. It took me considerably longer to replace one creative dream with another, to let go of my interest in drawing and to replace my paintbrush with a pen.

Epilogue

"You know you've been gone from the farm a long time when you get nostalgic about milking dairy cows," my sister said, shaking her head as she read one of my stories.

I chuckled. I guess that's right. Only time can soften the memory of getting up every single day at 5 a.m. Only time can turn milking cows into an event you joyfully anticipate. Only time can make you remember with fondness the cows that kicked in irritation whenever you attached a milking machine, leaving bruises all along your forearms. Only time can erase the feel and smell and taste of a manure-caked, rain-soaked cow tail slapping you in the face. Well, actually you may never forget that!

It's true my memories are made more beautiful by a golden glow that shines brightly on the positive, while shading the negatives with forgetfulness. But all the stories I've written are true, to me at least.

When Dad and Mom retired from the farm in the early 1970s, they asked me if I wanted to take over. Married for four years, with a child of my own, my life and career on another track, I said no. I return to that decision again and again, sometimes with regret, playing little 'what if' games in my head. More often I accept the reality of a husband who would never have been content in farm life. But always, yearnings tug at my heart. The farm life I lived with family close and values solid, always pulls me back. To me as a child, life was simple and pure. And I saw that life as best. It gave me the foundation to become a productive adult

I carried my ability to work hard, to be independent, to overcome challenges, into a successful career in public relations. I rechanneled my desire to be an artist from painting to writing. Most important, my family—parents, sisters and grandmothers—and the family values they taught helped me raise a good son into a fine man.

A wonderful childhood could not shield me from the tough stuff of life, particularly a painful divorce after 13 years of trying to hold my marriage together. But it did give me the tools, over time, to learn and grow from the experience. And I married again with optimism and a willingness to learn from my mistakes.

To this day, I enjoy creating something tangible with my hands—a farm-instilled value. Any day in which I bake cookies or dig in the garden or clean the house or trim the hedge is better than a day when I while away the hours reading. My husband and I garden, and I can and freeze the produce, but I acknowledge I will never keep up with my mother. At 91, she still put in a garden and ended the summer with fruit cellar shelves lined with pints and quarts of vegetables and fruits and meat she canned herself.

Someone asked me if kids growing up on farms today could have the kind of experience I did.

I hesitated. I wanted to say, sure. Kids still work on farms with their parents. Farm kids still absorb solid values working on the land.

But I stopped. After thinking about it for a

moment, I had to say, no. Farm life as I experienced it is slipping away by the day. A farm of 180 acres—the size of our farm—would be hard-pressed to support a family these days. Today's farmers manage thousands of acres instead of hundreds. In the late-1950s, some 1.8 million dairy farms dotted the landscape of the United States; dairy farmers were considered the backbone of the country. By 2007, that number dropped to 65,000.

The world has changed more than the 40 years that have passed since my years on the farm.

By the time I reached high school in the 1960s, the pace of change had accelerated. The Russians launched Sputnik and the space race shifted into high gear. Instead of a test pattern at midnight, television airs news 24/7. We watch wars fought in real time. The Internet and cell phones often make it easier to interact with someone halfway around the world than a family member in the next room.

So, no, even farm kids live in a radically different world than the one I experienced.

I also have to think my parents were unique. I still don't know how they made us see work as a gift. Whether in the barn milking the cows, in the garden planting radishes or potatoes, in the basement butchering chickens, they were there and we kids were there, each of us involved, each of us important, each of us truly valued.

I have only to close my eyes and breathe in to remember the smell of a field of new-mown hay, flex my fingers to remember the feel of a calf sucking as it learned to drink, open my ears to the sound of my mother smoothing over a cooking mistake. Then I remember my dad sitting on the feedbox petting a yellow tomcat and I want to go sit by him again and talk about the work that has yet to be done.

Growing Up Country:
Memories of an Iowa Farm Girl
Reader Discussion Guide

Overview
In this memoir, author Carol Bodensteiner shares stories about growing up on a family dairy farm in middle America in the middle of the 20th century.

Are you a member of a book group? Below are questions that will enliven your discussion.

Would you like the author to join your discussion? Carol enjoys sharing stories with book clubs. Though it is not always possible to be there in person, Skype and speakerphones are the next best thing. Contact Carol at www.carolbodenstiner. com to see what's possible.

Discussion questions

1.   Bodensteiner shares stories of everyday life living on a dairy farm. How does her experience growing up compare with your own? What are the benefits/detriments of "growing up country," compared to growing up in a small town, a city or the suburbs?

2.   Few Americans grow up on farms today and the culture of farm life in the 1950s may seem foreign. What do you find most surprising, intriguing or difficult to understand?

3.   In "I Bet You A Million Bucks," the author faces moral and ethical dilemmas when she loses a bet to a

classmate. What psychological tools did she have to handle this challenge? How effective were those tools?

4. Growing up on a dairy farm, the author spends a lot of time doing chores in the barn and in the house. Do you find her attitudes about hard work realistic? What happenings in her life made such an attitude possible?

5. When the author turns 10, her parents expect her to take on more responsibility, including cooking and carrying milk. Are their expectations reasonable? What do these expectations say about farm life? Childhood?

6. In today's society some have felt the amount of work these children were expected to handle bordered on abusive. Do you agree or disagree? Why?

7. Bodensteiner tells her stories of growing up country in the 1950s. How have advances in technology (television, computers, the Internet) changed the inner workings of the family as a unit? Have those changes had a positive or negative impact on the childhood experience?

8. Food played a major role in the author's family. Meals brought the family together and were part of the hospitality for guests. How have meals and family interaction changed since the 1950s? What role does food play in your family and in how you entertain guests?

9. In "Options" we see the author's parents' attitudes and approaches to healthcare. How do you react to her father's comment about education, "Paper don't care what you print on it"? How do you respond to her mother's apparent lack of concern regarding the doctor's advice?

10.   Participation in groups like 4-H was intended to teach many things. The author's shirt ironing demonstration taught her an unexpected lesson about fairness. What life lessons did you learn as a young person by participating in groups? Is it possible to pass on those lessons to your children/grandchildren to help guide them through life's challenges?

11.   Most chapters illustrate some value the author learned as a result of her childhood experiences. In what ways were the values she learned growing up similar to your own or different?

12.   What have you learned from reading this book? In what ways has it altered your perspective of the time period, farming or rural culture?

Go Away Home

Chapter 1—Iowa – 1913

A fly buzzed against her cheek, and Liddie brushed it away with the back of her hand, leaving a streak of flour in the sweat trickling down her temple. When a train whistle sounded in the distance, it triggered the dreams that were never far from her mind. She imagined standing on the platform, handing the porter her bag, stepping up into the car, and waving good-bye. The boldness of the idea thrilled her.

She sighed and turned her attention back to the bread dough. At sixteen, she dreamed of breaking away, of deciding her own future, of traveling, of doing anything but living on a farm. She wanted to see beyond the farthest rolling hill and start living her life. She hummed a wordless tune, matching her rhythm to the the pulse of the train chugging by on the tracks.

Grabbing a handful of flour from the bin, she spread it across the breadboard. She lifted the heavy gray crockery bowl and turned a small mountain of sticky dough onto the floured surface. Enough to make six big loaves. Enough to last the family a week. After coating her hands with more flour, she dusted it across the dough. Then she grasped the outside edge of the dough and pulled it into the center, pushing the mass in with the heels of her hands. Outside to inside; Brown's Station to Chicago. Outside to inside; Chicago to New York?

Carol Bodensteiner is a writer who finds inspiration in the people, places, culture and history of the United States Midwest. Born in Iowa and raised on her family's dairy farm, Carol grew up with a love of the land and an appreciation for family that form the foundation of her writing.

Carol blogs about her prairie, her family, gardening, writing, and whatever in life interests her at the moment. Her writing has been published in several anthologies. In addition to her memoir, Carol has published two novels: *Go Away Home,* a pre-WWI historical novel, and *Simple Truth,* a contemporary novel. Both are set in Iowa.

Carol lives with her husband on an acreage near Des Moines, Iowa.